SOCIAL EUROPE

One For All?

Monitoring European Integration 8

Centre for Economic Policy Research

The Centre for Economic Policy Research (CEPR) is a network of over 350 Research Fellows, based primarily in European universities. The Centre coordinates its Fellows' research activities and communicates their results to the public and private sectors. CEPR is an entrepreneur, developing research initiatives with the producers, consumers and sponsors of research. Established in 1983, CEPR is a European economics research organization with uniquely wide-ranging scope and activities.

CEPR is a registered educational charity. Institutional (core) finance for the Centre is provided by major grants from the Economic and Social Research Council, under which an ESRC Resource Centre operates within CEPR; the Esmée Fairbairn Charitable Trust; the Bank of England; the European Monetary Institute and the Bank for International Settlements; 21 national central banks and 42 companies. None of these organizations gives prior review to the Centre's publications, nor do they necessarily endorse the views expressed therein.

The Centre is pluralist and non-partisan, bringing economic research to bear on the analysis of medium- and long-run policy questions. CEPR research may include views on policy, but the Executive Committee of the Centre does not give prior review to its publications, and the Centre takes no institutional policy positions. The opinions expressed in this report are those of the authors and not those of the Centre for Economic Policy Research.

SOCIAL EUROPE

One For All?

Monitoring European Integration 8

Charles Bean
London School of Economics, and CEPR

Samuel Bentolila
CEMFI, Madrid, and CEPR

Giuseppe Bertola
*University of Turin, European University
Institute, Florence, and CEPR*

Juan Dolado
University Carlos III, Madrid, and CEPR

Centre for Economic Policy Research

90–98 Goswell Road
London
EC1V 7DB
UK

Tel: (44 171) 8782900
Fax: (44 171) 8782999
Email: cepr@cepr.org

© Centre for Economic Policy Research, 1998

British Library Cataloguing in Publication Data
A catalogue record for this book is available from the British Library

ISBN 1 89812833-2

Printed and bound in the UK

Contents

MEI Steering Committee   *page vii*
List of Figures   *viii*
List of Tables   *ix*
Preface   *xi*
Executive Summary   *xv*

1 EU Social Policy   1
1.1 Landmarks in EU social policy   2
1.2 How binding is EU social policy?   9
1.3 Regulations on worker mobility   13
1.4 Social policy and social protection   14
1.5 Taking stock   15

2 Economic Integration and the Distribution of Income   18
2.1 The gains from economic integration   19
2.2 No pain, no gain: economic integration and income
     distribution   21
2.3 Mobility of goods v. mobility of factors   24
2.4 The lessons   27

3 Social Policies in an International Context   28
3.1 What does social policy do?   28
3.2 The demand for protection: integration and social policy   31
3.3 The supply of protection   38
     3.3.1 Spillovers and the 'race-to-the-bottom':
            the case for coordination   38
     3.3.2 *Cuius regio, eius religio* and competition
            between rules: the case for diversity   42
3.4 Social protection: the balance of demand and supply   45

**4 Lessons from the Past: Trade, Foreign Direct
     Investment and Enlargements**   51
4.1 Foreign direct investment and the scope for social dumping   52
4.2 Past enlargements   56

4.2.1 Structural changes and accession 61
4.2.2 Employment and the role of changing policies
in the cohesion countries 64
4.2.3 Lessons 67
4.3 Enlargement to the East 68
4.3.1 CEEC experiences and prospects 70
4.3.2 A policy dilemma 73

5 Social Policy in the Next Millennium 79
5.1 Forces for change 79
5.1.1 Increased competition 79
5.1.2 Migration 82
5.1.3 Economic and Monetary Union 84
5.2 Looking ahead 87
5.2.1 Political equilibria and intra-European integration 87
5.2.2 Good and bad ideas for a Social Chapter 91
5.2.3 Enlargement to the East 92

6 Conclusions 97

Endnotes 100
References 105

MEI Steering Committee

Richard E Baldwin
Institut Universitaire de Hautes Études Internationales,
Genève, and CEPR

David Begg
Birkbeck College, London, and CEPR

Jean-Pierre Danthine
Université de Lausanne and CEPR

Francesco Giavazzi
IGIER, Università Bocconi, and CEPR

Jürgen von Hagen
Zentrum für Europäische Integrationsforschung,
Universität Bonn, Indiana University, and CEPR

Paul Seabright
University of Cambridge and CEPR

Alasdair Smith
University of Sussex and CEPR

Charles Wyplosz
Institut Universitaire de Hautes Études Internationales,
Genève, and CEPR

List of Figures

Figure 4.1   Employment growth rates (relative to EU core)   *page* 60
Figure 4.2   Unemployment rates (relative to EU core)   60

List of Boxes

Box 1.1   Milestones in European social policy   3
Box 3.1   'Specific' and 'general' social policies   32
Box 3.2   Social clauses, distribution and gains from trade   35
Box 3.3   Posted workers: a case study in economic integration
              and social policy   49
Box 4.1   Irish growth and FDI   62
Box 4.2   Poland on the road to the EU   76

List of Tables

Table 1.1 Working time regulation in the EU *page* 11
Table 1.2 Income and social protection expenditure in the EU 16
Table 4.1 Hourly labour costs in industry in the EU 53
Table 4.2 Main economic indicators for Social Cohesion countries 59
Table 4.3 Basic economic facts in Social Cohesion countries
at accession 61
Table 4.4 Basic economic facts in Central and Eastern European
countries (selected EU countries 1996) 69
Table 4.5 Net migration rates in Central and Eastern European
countries (annual averages 1990–6) 75
Table 5.1 Employment protection regulation in Central and
Eastern European countries 94
Table 5.2 Stages of adoption of the social *acquis* in Eastern
European countries 95

Preface

Informed discussion of European integration should be based on economic analysis which is rigorous, yet presented in a manner accessible to public- and private-sector policy-makers, their advisers and the wider economic policy community.

Monitoring European Integration aims to meet this objective, by providing an annual assessment of the progress of, and obstacles encountered by, economic integration in Europe. A rotating panel of CEPR Research Fellows meets periodically to select key issues, analyse them in detail, and highlight the policy implications of the analysis. The output of the panel's work is a short annual Report, for which they take joint responsibility.

This Report (the eighth in the series) provides a detailed analysis of European labour markets, and sets out specific recommendations for the design and implementation of social policies within the EU. The Report addresses many of the issues raised in the debate surrounding the Social Chapter of the Maastricht Treaty. Can member states continue to implement their own social policies at the national level or must responsibility pass to the EU level? Is 'social dumping' inevitable in the absence of a common EU social policy? If provisions are needed, should they take the form of minimal agreements, or should there be exceptions for particular countries? How should the circumstances of the potential new members from Central and Eastern Europe be taken into account when designing current EU directives concerning social policy? Is social dumping to be welcomed, as a healthy force which will oblige countries to lighten the excessive and damaging regulations they impose on their labour markets?

The prescience, analytical clarity and relevance of previous Reports in this series promise a fresh, illuminating approach, and I believe readers will find these expectations justified.

The first *MEI* Report, published in 1990, examined the impact of developments in Eastern Europe on the economies of Western

Europe and on the process of economic integration among them. Some of its key insights went against conventional (and even new) wisdom, yet have proved correct and prophetic – for example, the conclusion that German unification would entail a real appreciation of the Deutsche Mark in the short run.

The 1991 Report dealt with Economic and Monetary Union in the European Community, in particular the macroeconomic and microeconomic issues arising from the process leading to a single currency and a European Central Bank. The Report served as a guide to evaluating the Maastricht Treaty and as a text for interpreting developments in the EMS since August 1992. Again, the analysis in that Report has proved far-sighted and robust, in particular its concerns with the problems of transition to monetary union.

The third Report, published in 1992, analysed the political economy of enlargement of what is now the European Union, in particular the accession of the members of EFTA and the Central and East European Countries.

The fourth *MEI* Report, on subsidiarity, will serve for a long while as the fundamental study of this complex problem of political economy. It examines the application of the principle of subsidiarity to both the macroeconomic and the microeconomic policies of the Union. It shows where central intervention may be justified on economic grounds and where there is no such justification, although political and bureaucratic motivations may nevertheless result in intervention.

MEI 5 offers a new approach to the challenge of high unemployment in Europe. The Report argues that the repeated calls for deregulation as the solution to European unemployment are over-simplified and naive: the costs of regulation are not as high as they appear, nor are European labour markets as sclerotic as is commonly argued, nor are the differences with the United States as clear as conventional wisdom maintains. This naiveté extends to the politics of high unemployment: European societies simply do not appear ready, according to the Report, to sacrifice the advantages of high wages, benefits and job protection in order to fight high unemployment. The authors analyse this resistance to solutions and what can be done with incremental change.

MEI 6 was the first analysis of *Flexible Integration* as a principle for further development of the EU. The concept has since become the key to progress in the Intergovernmental Conference, and the CEPR report is justly regarded as a major innovative step in this process.

MEI 7, published last year, focuses on the final stage of transition to EMU – from the choice in May 1998 of the first group of countries to participate in the Monetary Union to the launch of EMU at the beginning of 1999. The Report argued that the transition was poorly understood, that many extant proposals for managing the transition had fatal flaws, and that finding a safer transition strategy was an urgent priority. Amazingly, decisions already made at Maastricht and Madrid precluded any certainty about conversion rates between the Euro and national currencies until EMU actually begins. Nevertheless, it was possible to preannounce bilateral conversion rates between the 'Ins'. *MEI* 7 recommended doing so immediately and on the basis of existing central parities in the ERM. The Report argued that it would then be possible credibly to adopt very wide bands during the transition, and that in comparison with other proposals – such as reversion to narrow bands, or floating without prior commitment to the end point – this strategy would not only be more robust to speculative attack, but also more likely to deliver appropriate initial competitiveness levels in EMU.

The Report had an important impact on policy discussions in Europe, and at a high-level meeting in Paris in December 1997, the Deputy Governor of the Banque de France publicly thanked CEPR for the Report, which he confirmed had been the basis for the 1998 transition strategy recently adopted by the Finance Ministers and Central Bank Governors.

The German Marshall Fund of the United States provided generous financial assistance which was instrumental in establishing the *Monitoring European Integration* series. We are also grateful to the Commission of the European Communities, whose Human Capital and Mobility programmes financed the Centre's research networks on 'Macroeconomics, Politics And Growth In Europe' (Contract Number: ERB CHRXCT930234) and on 'Product Market Integration, Labour Market Imperfections and European Competitiveness' (Contract Number: ERB CHRXCT930235); and to the Ford Foundation, which has supported much of the Centre's research on economic integration. This Report includes new research, but since it is written and published quickly so as to be relevant to ongoing policy processes, it must rest on a solid base of past fundamental and policy-oriented research. The authors and CEPR express their continuing thanks for the support of such research which has come from these bodies and all others that contribute to the Centre's funding.

The authors and CEPR are also grateful to Sue Chapman and Julia Newcomb, as well as other staff at CEPR whose patience and professionalism have been most helpful in the production of this Report.

None of these institutions or individuals is in any way associated with the content of the Report. The opinions expressed are those of the authors alone, and not of the institutions to which they are affiliated nor of CEPR, which takes no institutional policy positions. The Centre is extremely pleased, however, to offer to an outstanding group of European economists this forum for economic policy analysis.

Stephen Yeo
18 May, 1998

Executive Summary

The pervasive welfare states of the European nations and the frequent references to a 'social dimension' in the documents and treaties that underpin the European Union (EU) stand as eloquent testimony to the desire of people and governments to ameliorate the undesirable social consequences of economic life. Measures to address these concerns – social policy for short – can take a variety of forms, from workplace regulation, constraints on worker dismissal, through to income transfers in the form of unemployment benefits, pensions, and the like. Mostly, such social policy seeks to remedy market failures and to protect the relatively disadvantaged members of society from the consequences of their economic weakness. Sometimes, however, it perversely ends up protecting better off groups within society.

This report explores the interactions between social policy, broadly interpreted, and economic integration. The essential thrust of economic integration in its various forms, from trade liberalization to enhanced labour and capital mobility, can be summarized thus: economic integration, while generally a good thing, usually has adverse consequences for relatively inefficient producers. The interaction between social policy and economic integration then becomes particularly obvious whenever – as is likely to be the case – it is the poorer members of the EU countries who lose out from integration. In that case integration is likely to lead to demands for increased levels of social protection.

The effectiveness of national social policy is, however, also affected by the degree of economic integration, and coordination of policies is required if policies are to be effective. Otherwise governments may be able to use social policies strategically in order to benefit their own citizens at the expense of foreigners by offering less regulation and lower social protection in order to encourage inflows of capital – what is usually referred to as 'social dumping'. If unchecked this will result in lower levels of social protection all round. This could actually be a good thing, however, to the extent that current national social policies in Europe are ill-designed or fail to protect the most disadvantaged members of society.

Drawing on the lessons of past experience with EU integration, and the enlargement to include the poorer Mediterranean countries and Ireland, the report discusses the implementation of national and EU social policies in the context of the pressures brought about by the continued deepening of EU economic integration associated with the Single Market and the introduction of the Single Currency, as well as the consequences of enlargement to the East. This leads us to conclude that continued integration will accentuate the pressure both for reform, and for greater coordination/harmonization in social policy. Consequently EU-level policies, though not particularly binding at present, may become a more significant factor in future.

The report is structured as follows. Chapter 1 lays out the historical record regarding EU social policy, and discusses whether EU policies presently constrain national policies. Our discussion of the analytic issues then commences in Chapter 2 with a brief review of the interaction between economic integration and the distribution of income. Chapter 3 considers the implications of integration for both the demand and supply of social policies, together with the pros and cons of coordination or harmonization through common standards on the one hand and subsidiarity on the other. Chapter 4 reviews the experience with the enlargement of the Community to include Greece, Ireland, Portugal, and Spain, and draws some comparisons with the prospective enlargement of the EU to the East. Finally in Chapter 5, we draw the various strands together in looking at: the strains on Europe's inclusive welfare states resulting from competition, migration and the introduction of the Euro; the prospects for social policies beyond the Millennium; and the special problems posed by Eastern enlargement.

1 EU Social Policy

The Community and the Member States, having in mind fundamental social rights such as those set out in the European Social Charter signed at Turin on 18 October 1961 and in the 1989 Community Charter of the Fundamental Social Rights of Workers, shall have as their objectives the promotion of employment, improved living and working conditions, so as to make possible their harmonisation while the improvement is being maintained, proper social protection, dialogue between management and labour, the development of human resources with a view to lasting high employment and the combatting of exclusion.

To this end the Community and the Member States shall implement measures which take account of the diverse forms of national practices, in particular in the field of contractual relations, and the need to maintain the competitiveness of the Community economy.

They believe that such a development will ensue not only from the functioning of the common market, which will favour the harmonisation of social systems, but also from the procedures provided for in this Treaty and from the approximation of provisions laid down by law, regulation or administrative action.

(Treaty of Amsterdam, Article 117)

More than forty years ago, in March 1957, the heads of state of six countries (the Benelux, France, Italy and West Germany) gathered in Rome to sign the Treaty on the European Economic Community (EEC). The aim of the Treaty was to achieve a common market among those countries by preventing discrimination against the other member states in product markets, abolishing restrictions on factor movements within the area, and equalizing tariffs and quotas on trade with non-member states.[1] Over time, the European Community has steadily broadened its activity in several ways. First, it has grown from six to 15 members, through subsequent enlargements to include: the UK, Denmark and Ireland in 1973; Greece in 1981; Spain and Portugal in 1986; and, lastly, Austria, Finland and

Sweden in 1995. Second, Community powers have deepened. In particular, there was a major step forward in the degree of economic liberalization with the adoption of the Single Market programme in 1987, which sought to attain free mobility of goods, services, labour and capital by the end of 1992. Powers in areas such as agricultural and competition policy have also increased. Third, there has been a widening in the scope of Community activities. Most significant has been the increasing degree of monetary integration, through the creation of the European Monetary System in 1979 and the plan for Economic and Monetary Union contained in the Maastricht Treaty signed in 1992. As a result, 11 EU member countries will share a single currency, the Euro, as of 1 January 1999.

Widening in the scope of Community activities has occurred rather more slowly with regard to social issues. There was little progress in this area for many years and even now there is little by the way of an EU-wide social policy. In this chapter we set the stage for the rest of the report by reviewing the evolution of EU social policy, and its relationship to national regulations, with the aim of shedding light on the forces that have either favoured or retarded the development of a pan-European social policy. The economic and political logic underlying these ideas is then discussed in the subsequent two chapters.

1.1 Landmarks in EU social policy

European governments have always been reluctant to relinquish their powers regarding social policies. Although harmonization of social regulation was envisaged as a goal in the Treaty of Rome, unanimity was required for measures in this area, ensuring that little was in fact achieved. The idea of an EU social policy was revived in the mid-1980s as a response to increased integration resulting from the Single Market programme, and the enlargement of the European Community and the concomitant pressures for at least minimum labour standards. The extension of qualified majority voting to certain social areas in 1986 and 1992 led to some harmonization, but to this day the Social Chapter remains a something of paper tiger. This section discusses the key steps in the development of EU social policy in the labour area,[2] particularly those EU-wide regulations known collectively as the *acquis communautaire*.[3] A brief summary of the main milestones appears in Box 1.1.

Box 1.1 **Milestones in European social policy**

Treaty of Rome (1957)

- Workers' right to freedom of movement within Community borders (Art. 48) recognized, with special regard to social security for migrant workers (Arts. 51 and 121). Mutual recognition of diplomas (Art. 57).
- Improvement of working conditions sought, so as to make possible their harmonization, including approximation of national legal provisions (Art. 117). Harmonization sought regarding equal pay for equal work for men and women (Art. 119) and paid holiday schemes (Art. 120).

Directives and regulations:
- Freedom of movement (68/360, 1968), equal treatment of migrants (1612/68, 1968), social security for migrant workers (1408/71, 1971, and 574/72, 1972).

First Social Action Programme (1974)

- Equal pay between men and women (75/117, 1975).
- Employees' rights in the event of collective redundancies (75/129, 1975), transfers of firms (77/187, 1977) and bankruptcies (80/987, 1980).
- Health and safety at work (several).

Single European Act (1986)

- Qualified majority voting for measures securing workers' freedom of movement (Art. 49).
- Harmonization sought in health and safety at work, through qualified majority voting for directives stating minimum requirements (Art. 118A).
- European Commission invited to promote social dialogue at the European level (Art. 118B).

Second Social Action Programme – Social Charter (1989)

- Mutual recognition of higher education diplomas (89/48, 1989).
- Improvements in the safety and health at work (89/391, 1989).

continued

continued from page 3

- Free movement of persons (90/361, 1990).
- Obligation to inform employees in writing of the conditions of the employment contract (91/533, 1991).
- Collective redundancies (92/56, 1992) (amendment).
- Organization of working time (93/104/EC, 1993).
- Protection of young people at work, prohibiting work for anyone under the age of 15 and regulating work for persons aged 15–18 (94/33, 1994).

Agreement on Social Policy of the Maastricht Treaty (1992)

- Qualified majority voting for directives stating minimum requirements in the fields of working conditions, informing and consulting workers, equality between men and women in the labour market, and the integration of persons excluded from the labour market.
- UK opts out.

Directives:
- Establishment of European works councils in Community-scale undertakings (94/45, 1994).
- Workers' right to parental leave (96/34, 1996).
- Burden of proof in sex discrimination cases (97/80, 1997).
- Equal treatment for part-time workers (97/81, 1997).

Third Social Action Programme (1995)

- Temporary posting of workers to another member state (96/71, 1996).

Amsterdam Treaty (1997)

- Employment and proper social protection set as objectives of the EU.
- UK accepts Agreement on Social Policy, which becomes part of the Treaty of the EU (Art. 118A).

Note: Following EU conventions, directives are referenced as (year/number), while regulations are referenced as (number/year).

The debate on social dumping in the 1950s. The idea that harmonization of working conditions should advance in parallel with trade liberalization was intensively discussed prior to the Treaty of Rome. At that time there were essentially two views: the first held that harmonization was a natural consequence of trade liberalization; the other considered it to be a prerequisite. Three studies from 1956 exemplify that debate.[4] Albert Delpérée, a high-ranking official of the Organization for European Economic Cooperation (the forerunner of the OECD), drew a distinction between wage and non-wage costs, the latter being related to working conditions and industrial relations. He rejected wage harmonization as a prerequisite for establishing a common market, but argued for harmonization of working conditions to prevent 'social dumping'.

In contrast, a group of experts, headed by Bertil Ohlin (International Labour Office, 1956), argued that wage and non-wage labour costs would balance each other, so that it would make no sense to harmonize one specific element, such as working conditions, across countries. On the other hand, their report argued that there would be 'unfair competition' if workers' remuneration 'in one industry... were much lower than in other industries within the same country', in which case harmonization was desirable. Similarly, a report commissioned by the intergovernmental committee preparing the EEC, chaired by the Belgian foreign minister, Paul-Henri Spaak, distinguished between 'general' and 'specific' distortions to competition (Comité Intergouvernemental Crée par la Conférence de Messine, 1956). The former were argued to stem from differences in general economic conditions across countries and would not warrant any harmonization. Specific distortions, on the other hand, were defined as taking place when a given industry in one country suffered charges lower both than those prevailing on average in the rest of that country and those in the same industry in other countries, so long as those charges were not offset by other charges. Specific distortions would warrant harmonization, with examples given by 'the relationship between male and female wages, working hours, overtime rates, or paid holidays'. (The debate about the effects of 'specific' and 'general' social policies is revisited below in Chapter 3 in Box 3.1.)

The Treaty of Rome (1957). The Treaty essentially endorses the view of the Ohlin report: while calling for improved working conditions 'so as to make possible their harmonization' and allowing for the approximation of national laws, it contained no enforcement mechanism. Two areas in particular were singled out for harmonization: equal pay for equal work for men and women; and the maintenance of the existing equivalence between paid holiday schemes. The former was introduced at the insistence of the French, who already required it under national law, and feared foreign competition in industries employing a large fraction of female workers. Moreover, although the possibility of harmonization so as to eliminate specific distortions to competition is contemplated in the Treaty – and indeed has played a role in other areas – it has never been applied in the field of social policy.

In fact, little harmonization took place in the subsequent 15 years, even in the areas mentioned in the Treaty, for several reasons. First, there was no political consensus for harmonization, since only the French were actively in favour. Second, the prevailing environment of high growth and low unemployment muted the demands of workers and businesses for protection against imports. Third, there was a progressive convergence of labour costs among members of the common market reducing the pressure for protection against 'unfair' competition from low cost producers with lax standards (hourly industrial labour costs in the country with the lowest costs were just 58% of those of the country with the highest costs in 1958, but had risen to 70% by 1972). Lastly, integration involved mostly trade in similar products (intra-industry trade) which as we note below tends to raise fewer distributional issues.

The First Social Action Programme (1974). Political consensus emerged in the early 1970s for some sort of Community-wide social policy. Significant advances in social protection had been achieved in most countries by that time. In the wake of the first oil price shock, each government had an incentive to reduce the scope for regulatory competition from other members by harmonizing social regulations with them. This coincided with the ill-fated Werner Plan for economic and monetary union which, if implemented, would have intensified competition. These developments led, in 1974, to the First Social Action Programme. Directives were concentrated in three areas:

- *Equal treatment for men and women,* in regard to pay, access to employment, vocational training and promotion, working conditions and social security. These directives purported to eliminate all discrimination on grounds of sex, except for the protection of women (e.g. in respect of maternity). Excluding access, the objective was to achieve equality in outcome rather than merely of opportunities.

- *Labour law and working conditions*, in particular granting workers rights to be informed and consulted in the event of collective redundancies, transfers of firms or bankruptcies.

- *Health and safety at work*, with directives on chemical, physical and biological agents, accident hazards, asbestos, noise levels, etc.

The Single European Act (1986). Two key events regarding the development of the EU took place in the mid-1980s. First, the European Commission launched the Single Market programme, thus restarting the process of European integration after ten years of low growth and rising unemployment. This sought the elimination of all remaining barriers to the mobility both of goods and services, and of labour and capital, by the end of 1992. Second, two new countries entered the Community, namely Portugal and Spain. Together with two other recent entrants, Greece and Ireland, these countries had significantly lower per capita incomes and labour costs than the other members of the EU; for example, hourly industrial labour costs in Portugal in 1984 were just 17% of those in West Germany. As we will see in Chapters 2 and 3, both of these events – leading to increased competition in general, and from low cost, labour-rich/capital-poor countries in particular – could be expected to lead to an intensification of pressures for some coordination or harmonization in social policies. Joined to the social activism of the then President of the European Commission, Jacques Delors, they led to the addition of a *social dimension to the internal market*, within the framework of the Single European Act.

The Act relaxed the requirement of unanimity in favour of qualified majority voting in a number of areas. In social policy, this was applied to health and safety at work, singled out for ultimate harmonization, through directives setting minimum requirements for gradual implementation. In other areas, the European Commission was invited to promote dialogue between management and labour at the European level as an additional lever for harmonization.

The Commission then issued the Community Charter of the Fundamental Social Rights of Workers, or *Social Charter*[5], adopted in 1989 by all members bar the UK, with Prime Minister Margaret Thatcher arguing that she saw no need for common labour standards, favouring instead deregulation through 'competition among rules' (on which see our discussion below in Chapter 3). The Social Charter gave rise to a host of directives on health and safety, plus two other harmonization directives, one on the duty of employers to inform employees in writing of employment conditions, and another making the 1975 directive on collective redundancies more stringent. A directive was also approved banning work for anyone under the age of 15 (subject to a few exceptions) and regulating work for young persons between the ages of 15 and 18.

An additional joint consequence of the completion of the Single Market and enlargement was the decision to double the size of the Structural Funds, or sectoral subsidies, with the additional resources directed to the four poorest countries: Greece, Ireland, Portugal and Spain (the *Social Cohesion Countries*).

The Agreement on Social Policy in the Maastricht Treaty (1992) and the Social Chapter (1997). The next step towards social harmonization was taken at Maastricht with the attempt to include a 'Social Chapter' in the Treaty. Economic and Monetary Union represented a further significant step forward in integration and promoted renewed fears of 'social dumping' which the Social Chapter was designed to address. The UK vetoed this initiative, with Prime Minister John Major arguing that it would foster unnecessary EU intervention in social affairs. Instead, in a Protocol on Social Policy annexed to the Treaty, all 12 countries allowed 11 of them (i.e. excluding the UK) to sign an Agreement on Social Policy. The Agreement enlarged the scope for harmonization by extending qualified majority voting to several new areas: working conditions; information and consultation of workers; equality between men and women in the labour market; and the integration of persons excluded from the labour market. Again, this would take place through directives stating minimum requirements for gradual implementation. The scope of harmonization was limited by requiring that directives should have 'regard to the conditions and technical rules obtaining in each of the Member States' and should 'avoid imposing administrative, financial and legal constraints' on small and medium-sized firms.

This Agreement finally became the Social Chapter in 1997, when the new Labour administration under Prime Minister Tony Blair ended the British opt-out in the Amsterdam revision of the Maastricht Treaty. This is the main novelty regarding social policy in the Treaty, which also includes the promotion of employment and 'proper social protection' as objectives of the Community, but without allowing for qualified majority voting to attain them.

The Social Chapter led to the adoption of four directives:

- The European works councils directive which gives workers' representatives in multinational companies with at least a thousand employees within member states and at least 150 employees in each of at least two member states (so-called 'Community-scale undertakings'), the right to be informed and consulted on management decisions through formal works councils or equivalent procedures.

- The parental leave directive which guarantees workers of either sex minimum unpaid leave of three months due to the birth or adoption of a child, while keeping all their existing job rights.

- The directive on equal treatment for part-time employees which grants them non-discriminatory treatment *vis-à-vis* full-time workers through the proportionality of pay and benefits to time at work.

- The directive concerning sex discrimination at the workplace which states that once a plaintiff has established a *prima facie* case of sex discrimination, the employer is obliged to justify not having acted in a discriminatory manner.

1.2 How binding is EU social policy?

Starting in the 1950s, most European countries developed an extensive network of regulations to protect workers in respect of issues such as discrimination, job security, hours of work, collective bargaining and strikes. As with social security, the demand for such regulations is in part the natural consequence of higher incomes as security is usually a superior good, presumably because individuals have more to lose when they are well off. Regulations were significantly strengthened in the 1970s, in the wake of the oil price shocks, although the last decade and a half have witnessed a slow rolling back of some of these regulations, in the wake of business demands for increased flexibility and a realization that they inhibited employment and growth. Legal provisions and collective bargaining practices have led to much more regulated labour markets in the EU than in the US, for example. Still, the degree of restrictiveness varies significantly across EU countries, with the UK, Denmark and Ireland on the low side, and Portugal, Greece and Spain on the high side.[6]

How does EU social policy compare with the national regulations operating in individual countries? First, most EU directives are generally much less stringent than existing national laws. This can be illustrated with regard to three fields:

- *Work-force participation in business decisions.* National industrial relations systems differ greatly across EU countries, not only in terms of the legal framework, but also along dimensions such as unionization rates and the degree of centralization/coordination in wage bargaining.[7] Thus, there seems to be little chance that European Commission proposals in this field, discussed on and off for the last 20 years, will ever be adopted. The main role played by the EU in this area has been in fostering a dialogue between the Union of Industrial and Employers' Confederations of Europe (UNICE) and the European Trade Unions Confederation (ETUC), and the only consequence to date has been their agreement to the 1997 directive granting (proportionately) equal treatment to part-time employees in respect of pay and other benefits as to full-timers.

- *Employment protection.* Whereas all EU countries have quite stringent regulations of individual dismissals,[8] there are none so far at the EU level (they have been proposed, but so far rejected). There are, however, EU regulations regarding collective dismissals (defined as dismissal of roughly 10% or more of a firm's employees over any 30-day period[9]): management must consult workers' representatives, supplying them with information on the circumstances of the redundancies, and notify the relevant labour authorities. All EU countries have even stricter regulations, however.[10] For example, the labour authorities may ban redundancies in Greece, the Netherlands and Spain (and also in France before 1986), and most countries also have minimum redundancy pay requirements. A related area in which there are national regulations, but proposed directives have failed to win support, is the protection of employees on 'atypical' contracts, i.e. fixed-term, agency and seasonal.

- *Hours of work.* A directive on maximum working time was adopted in 1993, although against the opposition of the UK. It guarantees workers minimum daily and weekly rest periods, maximum weekly working time (48 hours) and minimum paid annual leave (four weeks), as well as containing special provisions on night work. As Table 1.1 shows, directive levels were less restrictive than national ones in all countries except the UK, which had no law in this area. Moreover, the observed levels are in any case far below/above the national legal maxima/minima in all countries, so that EU directives are hardly likely to be a significant constraint in most labour contracts. Lastly, the directive in any case contains plenty of derogations regarding sensitive sectors where long hours, etc., might be natural (though its extension to such excluded occupations is presently under discussion).

Table 1.1 Working time regulation in the EU[1]

	Minimum daily rest (hours)	Minimum weekly rest (hours)	Maximum work week over a month (hours)	Average, usual work week (hours)	Employees with usual work week above 45 (hours(%))[2]	Minimum paid annual leave (weeks) Legislated	Collective agreements
EU 1993 directive	11	24	48	—	—	4	—
Belgium	15	24	45	38.1	3	4	5
Denmark	11	35	45	39.1	6	5	—
France	14	24	48	39.9	8	5	5.1
Germany	14	24	48	40.3	7	3	5.4
Greece	15	—	48	40.0	12	4	4.4
Ireland	13	24	48	40.5	11	3	4
Italy	16	24	48	38.6	8	4	—
Netherlands	14.5	24	45	39.1	3	4	4.7
Portugal	15	24	48	42.0	9	4.4	4.4
Spain	15	36	49.5	40.7	8	5	5
United Kingdom	—	—	—	43.6	30	—	—

[1] Circa 1993. Maxima and minima refer to constraints imposed by legislation, except for the last column. '—' means not applicable.
[2] Full-time employees.

Sources: Grubb and Wells (1993), Tables (columns): 3.C (2), 3 (8), 3.C (6), 7 (1,3), 3.A (1,2). For Spain in 1984, *Year Book of Labour Statistics,* International Labour Organisation, 1994.

Second, even when EU-wide norms exist and bite, implementation into national law and enforcement is frequently not straightforward. As of end-1993, of all the directives applicable to employment and social policy, Italy had transposed only 57% into national law, Luxembourg 59%, Greece 67% and Spain 68%, although at the other extreme Portugal and the UK had both transposed 92% of them.[11] To take a specific example, Italy did not implement the employment protection directive of 1975 until as late as 1993, and has yet to implement the hours of work directive of 1993. In both cases the European Court of Justice initiated proceedings against the Italian government, and in both cases the delay did not arise from the stringency of the provisions. Rather, it was politically difficult for the Italian government to implement clear legislation in socially sensitive fields which are otherwise regulated by union contracts and implicit, rather than explicit, rules and conventions. The current hours of work directive, for example, is mired in the whole 35-hours debate. Debate is *not* centred around the lower bound to be imposed under the EU directive; rather, it is about the extent to which the Italian legislation should be more stringent than is called for by the directive, with the extreme left insisting on working-time reduction beyond the current, largely informal status quo, and business organizations arguing for the legislation to make current contractual practices explicit.

As to enforcement, the mechanisms are weak. For example, the principle of equal pay for male and female workers is the only social harmonization principle cast in stone in Community law since the Treaty of Rome. Moreover, the European Court of Justice, whose rulings are binding on member states, solemnly sanctioned it as far back as 1976.[12] Nevertheless, it is not rigorously enforced, although that does not mean it is entirely inconsequential. For example, European countries have smaller wage differentials between men and women than the US, although there are large disparities across countries.[13] On more subtle grounds, enforcement of laws is often inversely related to their nominal stringency (e.g. French drink-driving laws are nominally more stringent than British ones, but are far less strictly enforced). Enforcement also tends to be looser where a given norm is more binding, as in that case the economic gains from loose observance will be greater and the norms are themselves likely to seem less reasonable.

<u>1.3</u> Regulations on worker mobility

The EU recognizes the free movement of persons as a fundamental right, along with the free movement of goods, services and capital. This right to freedom of movement of workers, included in the Treaty of Rome, is a separate force that makes labour policy coordination, if not harmonization, desirable. The right to work in another EU country under the same conditions as nationals, including the right to move within EU territory to seek work, and the right to stay in any EU country, was established as long ago as 1968.

Free movement of persons also requires the aggregation of any rights to social security benefits that migrant workers may obtain in separate countries, so that workers are not penalized as a result of moving country; moreover, benefits must be payable wherever workers may choose to reside. These rights were recognized in 1971–2. For example, upon reaching retirement age, a worker is entitled to one old-age pension for each country where he has been insured for at least one year, with the amount calculated according to each country's own insurance system, and the total number of years over which the worker has contributed to any of the national systems being appropriately taken into account. Thus, suppose a worker has worked for 30 years in Country A and then moved to Country B where he worked for 10 years before retiring. Country A will then pay 30/40 (three-fourths) of the amount corresponding to a worker having been insured there for 40 years, while the latter country will pay 10/40 (one-fourth) of the corresponding amount within its own system. The amount payable by all countries, however, may not be less than the minimum amount provided for in the legislation of the country of residence, when it is liable to pay a pension; for instance in the example if the retirement age is 67 in Country A and 60 in Country B, the retiree will not be eligible to draw the pension from Country A for another seven years and his resulting income may push him below the stipulated minimum. This latter provision is an incentive to 'pension shop', with workers choosing to spend the last years of their working life in countries with generous pension provisions.

Rules on the portability of unemployment benefits are, on the other hand, much more restrictive. A worker can only apply for benefits in their country of residence, i.e. the one in which the *last* job was held, and benefits follow the rules there. Moreover, after losing a job, the worker must remain at least one month in that country.

Benefits can be paid in another country only once between two periods of employment, and then for a maximum of three months. The worker may continue receiving benefits in the country of residence only if they return there at the end of the three months, although periods of contribution in other countries are at least taken into account in the calculation of entitlements.

The mutual recognition of national qualifications and diplomas is also desirable for labour mobility. This was already contemplated in the Treaty of Rome for the self-employed, but a case-by-case approach was followed, with the meticulous spelling out of requirements for mutual recognition. This allowed the generally self-regulating national professional associations to lobby their national governments for continued restrictions on entry, on the grounds of 'protecting the consumer' but effectively enabling them to keep wages in those professions high. Action at the EU level may help to reduce such barriers, as it allows governments to shelter behind the argument that 'Europe requires us to do this, so we have no choice'. Since 1989 there has indeed been some progress, with a directive promoting mutual recognition of higher education diplomas; also, vocational education is now being promoted at the EU level to facilitate mobility. Nevertheless, there is, as yet, no EU-wide accreditation system for schools or universities and informal barriers persist.[14] As a result, between 1991 and 1994, only 10,000 EU citizens took advantage of the mutual recognition of their qualifications under the existing general system, and currently only around 5,000 take advantage each year of recognition under sectoral directives for doctors, dentists, architects, etc.[15]

1.4 Social policy and social protection

So far we have identified social policy with labour market regulation, but social policy in the broad sense obviously includes expenditure on social programmes too. Social protection is very largely carried out by individual countries, not by the EU. The European Social Fund, which itself consumes only 9% of the total EU budget, or around just 0.1% of total EU GDP, finances mainly education, training and job placement, not social spending. It is true that the rest of the EU budget, such as the Common Agricultural Policy and the rest of the Structural Funds, though not strictly speaking social spending may nevertheless be considered as serving a social role. Even so the whole EU budget still amounts to only 1.3% of EU GDP, so this does not change the picture very much.

The citizens of Europe generally appear to have a strong preference for social protection. Among the 12 countries which were members of the EU prior to 1995 (the EU12), social protection expenditure in 1994 averaged 29% of GDP.[16] The entry of Austria, Finland and Sweden in 1995 has further raised that figure. This is in contrast to other rich countries, like Canada, the US and Japan, which have much lower spending on social protection. Within the EU, expenditure shares vary widely, ranging from 16% in Greece to 35% in Finland (see Table 1.2). The Cohesion countries all spend less than a quarter of GDP, whereas the remaining countries spend more. Since income per head, however, is also lower in the poor countries, the disparities become even starker when judged in terms of the absolute level of expenditure per head (at comparable purchasing power), with Luxembourg, at the top, spending four times more than Greece, at the bottom.

As to the composition of this spending, old-age pensions take the lion's share (44%), followed by sickness and invalidity pensions (35%), unemployment benefits (9%) and family benefits (8%) (see Table 1.2). The sources of finance for these expenditures are employers' social contributions, either actual (28%) or imputed (11%), followed by taxpayers in general (30%) and the protected persons themselves (25%). There is wide variation across countries in both expenditure and financing shares. This is mainly the result of differences in social protection system design, which moves along a continuum between two polar models. In the 'Beveridge' system, benefits are a citizen's right, are paid as a flat rate and are financed through taxes. In the 'Bismarkian' system, contributions provide access to and financing of benefits, which are earnings-related. Scandinavian countries roughly adhere to the first system, and Austria, Benelux, France and Germany to the second, with the remaining EU members placed somewhere in between.

1.5 Taking stock

What can we infer about the factors that have favoured or retarded the development of an EU-wide social policy? The events surveyed in this chapter suggest to us the following. Over the last 40 years the members of the EU have become more integrated, both through

Table 1.2 Income and social protection expenditure in the EU

	GDP/head in 1994 at PPS[1] (EU12 = 100)	Social protection expenditure in 1994 (% of GDP)	Benefits by function as a % of total benefits (1993)				
			Sickness/invalidity/ occupational accidents	Old age/ survivors	Family/ maternity	Unemployment/ employment promotion	Other
Belgium	110.4	27.0	34.5	44.3	8.4	11.4	1.4
Denmark	110.6	33.7	28.1	34.0	11.8	18.9	7.2
France	107.8	30.5	34.1	43.5	9.6	8.3	4.6
West Germany	123.3	27.7	40.1	41.2	7.7	7.8	3.3
Germany	—	30.8	38.4	40.8	8.0	9.7	3.2
Greece	61.8	16.0	24.2	66.6	1.4	3.4	4.5
Ireland	78.9	21.1	37.1	28.1	12.7	17.0	5.2
Italy	99.3	25.3	31.0	63.0	3.7	2.3	0.0
Luxembourg	168.4	24.9	39.3	46.8	12.6	1.0	0.3
Netherlands	103.6	32.3	44.5	37.0	5.4	9.2	3.8
Portugal	63.3	19.5	44.5	40.6	5.4	6.5	2.9
Spain	74.8	23.6	35.5	40.5	1.7	21.0	1.4
United Kingdom	97.8	28.1	31.3	41.3	11.4	7.3	8.6
EU12 (1990)[2]	100.0	27.6	35.5	44.6	7.6	8.4	3.9
EU12	—	28.6	35.2	44.3	7.8	9.0	3.8
Austria	113.4	30.2	—	—	—	—	—
Finland	89.9	34.8	—	—	—	—	—
Sweden	97.2	—	—	—	—	—	—

[1] Purchasing Power Standard specific to private consumption.

[2] 'EU12 (1990)' refers to the old territorial situation of the EU with 12 member states, without the new German Länder. EU12 includes the latter.

Source: Eurostat, Social Protection Expenditure and Receipts 1980–94, 1997. Col. 1: Tables D.1, D.2 and D4. Col. 2, Table B1. Col. 3. Table B7.

increased trade in goods and services, and through increased mobility of capital (through both portfolio and foreign direct investment); see Chapter 5 for more discussion on this. We have seen that the major movements forward in economic integration have frequently coincided with new attempts at developing some form of harmonization of social policies in the EU, a fact which is suggestive of a causal relationship between the two. Two other recent developments are also potentially relevant: increased income heterogeneity as integration proceeds; and increases in unemployment in most member states. The timing of events presented above suggest that these three elements have come hand-in-hand with renewed efforts to develop a pan-European social policy.

We have also seen that the original debate in the 1950s as to whether social policy harmonization was a precondition, or a consequence, of economic integration was *de facto* resolved in favour of the latter. Moreover, and quite strikingly, the fact that individual country social security systems have become highly developed and labour market regulations very restrictive has not been associated with a closing of the gap between pan-European and individual country policies. As a result, progress in developing EU social policy has been slow – indeed much slower – than in other areas such as trade or monetary policy.

Having outlined the historical experience, we now need to delve deeper into the logic – both economic and political – which underlies the desire for an EU social policy to accompany economic integration. This is the task of the next two chapters, which draw on both the basic economic theory of international trade and ideas from political economy. We then return to the European experience, link theory to the facts, draw conclusions about likely future developments in this area, and make a number of policy recommendations.

2 Economic Integration and the Distribution of Income

It is quite as important to the happiness of mankind, that our enjoyments should be increased by a better distribution of labour, by each country producing those commodities for which by its situation, its climate, and its other natural or artificial advantages, it is adapted, and by their exchanging them for the commodities of other countries, as that they should be augmented by a rise in the rate of profits... It has been my endeavour to shew [sic] throughout this work, that the rate of profits can never be increased but by a fall in wages.

('On Foreign Trade', David Ricardo, *On the Principles of Political Economy and Taxation*, Ch.VII, p.132 in Sraffa (1951)).

One cannot begin to understand whether charges of social dumping are justified or not without first understanding the relationship between trade in goods and factor mobility on the one hand, and welfare and the distribution of income on the other. This chapter briefly reviews this relationship. Chapter 3 then uses the analysis to illuminate how integration interacts with the implementation of national social policies. Readers familiar with the standard theory of trade and distribution and impatient to get to that discussion may therefore move swiftly on to Chapter 3.

Warlike metaphors about the 'threat' posed by competition from other countries pepper the speeches of politicians when they talk, and the columns of journalists when they write, about economic integration, globalization and the like. Yet, as any economist will point out, economic integration should not reduce economic efficiency. Quite simply, any pattern of production and consumption that was feasible before integration still remains feasible when countries can trade and/or factors of production relocate. In a market economy, trade and factor mobility should be seen as opportunities, not obligations, and taking advantage of them should be expected to increase aggregate welfare. Such developments – like all change – are, however, typically associated with changes to the distribution of income and wealth, and it is this that is at the root of so much hostility to integration and the calls for the protection of social standards. In this chapter we concentrate attention on examining why – efficiency gains notwithstanding – trade liberalization typically encounters so much opposition. First, however, we need to briefly remind the reader of the reasoning that leads one to expect free trade to raise potential welfare.

2.1 The gains from economic integration

If countries and individuals were all identical there would be no reason for them to trade with each other, for the gains from trade result from the scope for specialization that arises from differences in technologies, tastes or endowments. The classic theory of comparative advantage focuses on differences in technological possibilities across goods and countries. For example, the cost of producing shoes may be lower in Italy than in the UK, while the opposite may be true for, say, financial services. In this context, the relevant 'cost' notion is one of foregone *opportunity*. Suppose that a unit of Italian labour would forego one unit of financial services production to produce a pair of shoes, while the amount of labour needed to produce a pair of shoes in the UK would yield more than one unit of financial services if it were so employed. Then, the UK has a *comparative* advantage in the production of financial services and Italy has a comparative advantage in shoe production. Since it takes less labour to produce any given bundle of shoes and financial services when production of the former is concentrated in Italy and that of the latter is concentrated in the UK, and as long as consumption of the two goods is not similarly concentrated, an efficient allocation of production obtains only when trade and specialization are allowed. If trade is impossible (autarky), then both British and Italian workers will be able to purchase fewer financial services and fewer shoes with their labour.[17]

It is important to bear in mind here that technological differences may well be such as to make one country's labour less productive in *both* industries; for example, a sunnier disposition and healthier lifestyle may make it easier for Italians than for the British to produce both financial services and shoes. This means that Italian workers enjoy an *absolute* technological advantage, and will be able to consume larger quantities of both goods than the British. While this is no doubt an unfortunate state of affairs for the British, it should not be blamed on trade, for similar income comparisons could also be made under autarky. Similarly, trade can hardly be expected to make the British richer than Italians, if the opposite was true before integration. The relevant comparison thus should always be between each worker's standard of living with, and without, trade, not between different workers in different countries. In this world, economic integration makes everybody better off: the rich become richer and the poor become less poor, when the comparative technological advantage of their trading partners becomes available to them.

This reasoning relies on the existence of productivity differences between countries. Such differences are important in practice, and may derive from natural endowments (as in Ricardo's original example of sunny Portugal as a naturally privileged producer of wine and coal-rich England as a producer of manufactured goods) or on less obvious features of countries' technological know-how and institutions. It is unsatisfactory, however, to leave unexplained such an essential element of the theory when discussing trade in shoes and financial services, where production may be organized similarly in all locations and natural endowments presumably play a minor role as a source of comparative advantage.

Such considerations lead to another, although related, source of gains from specialization and trade, namely international differences in the comparative abundance of different factors of production. Even when the same technology is available to all countries, the UK may be more plentifully endowed with crafty accountants, while fashion designers may be less scarce in Italy. Standard economic theory then predicts that production in the UK should be relatively concentrated in the financial-services sector, while Italy should find it efficient to employ its designers in shoe production. Again, such specialization in the pattern of production will be associated with trade flows (with the UK exporting financial services and importing shoes), except in the rather unlikely event that consumer tastes in each country also happen to be sufficiently skewed towards the goods in which that country specializes. Trade will benefit all consumers, for a unit of income (no longer defined purely in terms of a single sort of labour) will now purchase more consumption goods than previously. Furthermore, this will be true regardless of how much richer one country's consumers are than those of the other.

A third source of gains from economic integration requires diversity in neither technologies nor factor endowments, but instead rests on the exploitation of economies of scale – in other words a tendency for average production costs to decline, rather than increase, with the level of production. If there are economies of scale then it makes sense for countries to concentrate in a few industries, and the pattern of concentration may be to a large extent indeterminate and driven by historical factors and happenstance rather than by technology or factor endowments.

Economies of scale can also be important within industries producing goods which, while similar in a fundamental sense, are nevertheless differentiated. The automobile industry is an obvious example. All cars serve the basic purpose of carrying people, but each model does so at different speeds and in different styles. Since the design and assembly-line costs of each model are fixed, producers will need to sell enough cars at a large enough margin over marginal costs if they are to break even; and prices can indeed exceed marginal costs since consumers view cars as imperfectly substitutable to each other, i.e. the car market displays a 'taste for variety'. By increasing the total size of the car market, economic integration widens the range of car shapes and styles on offer and, since more or less sharply differentiated car models may well be produced in different countries, variety effects can explain why countries may trade in similar goods, rather than in completely different goods as predicted by standard models of trade. This so-called 'intra-industry' trade is most relevant when similar rather than dissimilar economies are integrated, hence it is important in understanding the nature of trade within the 'core' countries of the EU, most of which is in manufactured goods.[18]

2.2 No pain, no gain: economic integration and income distribution

In all the theories sketched above, the gains from international trade accrue through lower goods prices, and changes in goods prices change the purchasing power of factor rewards. Now it is really the *potential* for, rather than the actuality of, trade that generates the downward competitive pressure on factor prices and costs. Hence, the essence of economic integration is really just a matter of enforcing the law of one price and ensuring that competition works to the advantage of the cheapest producer, and thus also to all consumers.

Seen from this perspective, it would be absurd ever to dislike trade because foreign goods or foreign labour are 'too cheap': trade, factor mobility and increased competitive pressure are beneficial precisely because they make cheaper goods available to *all* consumers in *all* countries involved in trade.

Since, however, trade affects factor incomes as well as goods prices, economic integration makes *all* individuals better off only in rather special circumstances. When trade opportunities arise from differences in technologies, all workers would unambiguously gain from trade if they were all alike and could freely move from one industry to another. The identity of each worker would then be completely immaterial, and with access to the technological possibilities of the other country everyone would necessarily enjoy higher consumption. Unfortunately, units of labour and other factors of production are in practice not alike, and at the same time as economic integration increases the size of the economic 'pie', it also tends to affect how it is shared out. For instance in our example, workers who used to produce shoes in the UK may find it difficult to learn how to produce financial services; if they bear the retraining costs rather than society at large, nothing guarantees that the price of consumption goods will fall sufficiently under free trade to let them afford even the consumption levels they achieved under autarky.

In passing it is worth noting that the effects of competition from foreign factors through trade are in many ways similar to those of competition from new machines as a result of technological progress.[19] Thus, Ned Ludd and his fellow workers who smashed up the latest textile machines in early nineteenth-century Britain were acting entirely rationally. These machines, while making possible cheaper clothes for the population at large, also brought about a reduction in the manpower required in textile production. Similarly, manufacturing workers in the US and the EU who find themselves displaced by cheaper manufactures imported from the Far East or Eastern Europe will regret the dismantling of trade barriers that makes what they used to produce more affordable to their countrymen. From the point of view of a displaced worker, imports are indeed 'too cheap', just as the new textile machines were 'too productive' to the Luddites.

When based on differences in factor endowments rather than technologies, trade will generally raise (lower) the rewards of factors that are in relatively abundant (scarce) supply. These movements in factor rewards are guaranteed to afford higher consumption to a mythical 'representative' individual who owns factors in the same proportions as the economy as a whole. They will, however, tend to decrease the income of individuals who own a disproportionately large share of the factor that is initially relatively scarce. To focus on the impact of economic integration on income distribution in the current context, it is perhaps most helpful to think of the two factors concerned as 'skilled' and 'unskilled' labour, with skilled labour earning a higher income than unskilled labour, both before and after economic integration.

Consider then the distributional implications of economic integration between a 'rich' country that is relatively well endowed with skilled labour, and a 'poor' country that is relatively well endowed with unskilled labour. Since skilled labour is less scarce in the integrated economy than in the poor country, and the opposite is true of unskilled labour, income differentials within the poor country should be narrowed by economic integration. Similarly, unskilled labour will be less scarce in the integrated economy than within the rich country alone; hence, income differentials must widen there. As a result of the more efficient pattern of production under integration, we can definitely say that the skilled in the rich country and the unskilled in the poor country are absolutely, as well as relatively, better off. The unskilled in the rich country and the skilled in the poor country may, however, be either absolutely better or worse off, depending on whether the gains from lower consumer prices outweigh the decline in their incomes.

In summary, when high-income factors are more abundant in rich countries than in poor countries, then trade opportunities based on differences in factor endowments can be expected to *reduce* income inequality within poor countries and *increase* inequality in rich countries. This unambiguous prediction looms large in policy debates, and much recent empirical work has aimed at assessing its empirical relevance.[20] Increased income inequality – especially in the US and the UK – did coincide with more intense 'globalization' during the 1980s and 1990s. At the same time, however, technological innovation and institutional changes[21] also raised the demand for skilled labour. While these coincident trends make it hard to pin down precisely the empirical relevance of economic integration for trends in wage inequality, trade cannot be completely dismissed as a source of greater income inequality in developed countries. Furthermore, even though the statistical evidence may be inconclusive, the issues are clear enough in the minds of policy-makers and workers under threat from foreign competition.

While we have set the discussion in terms of skilled and unskilled labour, similar reasoning applies to other factor incomes. Most importantly, the argument can be applied to the classic case where the two factors of production are capital and (undifferentiated) labour. Suppose, plausibly, that the 'rich' country is relatively well endowed with capital and the 'poor' country with labour, and suppose realistically[22] that individuals with high incomes in each country also tend to own proportionately more capital. Then rich (capitalist) individuals within the rich country can take advantage of the greater relative scarcity of capital in the integrated economy, while their poorer (worker) compatriots face an effective increase in the relative abundance of labour: once again, inequality increases within the rich country and decreases in the poor country. In addition the degree of income inequality *between* the two countries (as measured by average *per capita* income) declines, while everybody benefits from the lower prices afforded by the more efficient pattern of specialization.

The distributional implications of integration for the other main motivation for trade – the advantages of diversity – are not clear cut and relate to possible increases in competitive pressure arising within previously segmented markets. In this respect, the role of economic integration is akin to that of competition policies that reduce monopoly power within (rather than across) countries. Just as anti-trust policies enhance efficiency and benefit consumers as they simultaneously deprive monopolists of their excess profits, so economic integration increases competition from foreign producers of similar goods, intensifies intra-industry trade, and redistributes incomes across producers and consumers. These issues are important in the current European context, but are not central to this report's focus, which is not so much on the effects of deeper integration within the 'core' of the EU, but rather on the impact of increased integration with the poorer countries of the Mediterranean and Eastern Europe, as well as with the rest of the world.

2.3 Mobility of goods v. mobility of factors

An important question is whether migration of labour or capital can ever substitute for international movements in goods. The migration of factors will be driven by the differences in the return a given factor can earn across regions, not the relative returns to *different* factors within a region – in other words what matters to workers is not the wage relative to the return to capital in their own country, but rather their wage relative to the wage they could get by moving abroad (and similarly for capital, *mutatis mutandis*). So, when comparative advantage is based purely on technological differences between countries, factor mobility cannot help the residents of one region reap the reward of the comparative advantage of the other. Conversely, absolute advantages of production in each location are a powerful motive for migration, and no amount of trade will ever let individuals living in a disadvantaged location earn the same income as if they moved to a country where production is easier. Hence, when technological differences are the source of gains from economic integration then migration and trade are complements rather than substitutes.[23]

By contrast when relative factor abundance is the main source of the gains from economic integration, labour migration or flows of capital can play much the same role as trade in goods. Consider our example of a rich and a poor country, with the rich country being relatively well endowed with capital, and *vice versa*. Then the two economies can be integrated just as well by capital moving from the rich country (where capital is abundant) to the poor country (where capital is scarce, and hence the return to capital higher), as by free trade in goods and services (which, if fully exploited, implies that factors of production earn the same regardless of their location).

Factor mobility, therefore, has implications for the distribution of income that are similar to trade. Thus, if capital rather than goods become mobile, with capital flowing to the poor country to take advantage of the abundant and cheap labour, then owners of capital in the rich country, as well as workers in the poor country, will find themselves becoming relatively better off, while the owners of capital in the poor country and workers in the rich country are relatively worse off, just as they would be with integration through trade. In addition, everybody will enjoy the efficiency gains afforded by a more efficient matching of capital to labour in the integrated economy; this may, but need not, ensure that even the owners of capital in the poor country and workers in the rich country are absolutely better off.

Trade and factor mobility need not be such close substitutes when the gains from economic integration are not based on differences in factor endowments. To bring our simple examples closer to reality we should recognize that 'rich' countries typically enjoy an absolute productivity advantage, in the sense that the same amounts of capital and labour would usually yield more output there than in a poor country. Thus, technological know-how, geographical features and cultural and institutional characteristics make Germany a more hospitable location for production of a wide variety of goods than, say, the Gobi desert, Libya or even maybe Poland, regardless of the current (and potentially changeable) endowments of labour and capital in those regions. Any such absolute advantage may reverse the direction of factor flows predicted by reasoning based on standard relative factor endowments: capital, for example, may well flow out of Russia and into Switzerland, despite its obvious scarcity in the former and abundance in the latter.

Furthermore, an absolute advantage in production and differences in other amenities can trigger the mobility of factors other than capital, over and above that called for by relative factor endowments. Individuals can and do move in response to economic incentives where this is possible. Migration from less to more productive locations should, of course, tend to increase aggregate production (net of moving costs) but, just like the movement of goods and capital, it has implications for the distribution of income as well as economic efficiency.

In general, factors that are substitutes for the one that migrates will gain in their country of origin, and lose in the host country. Now there are good reasons to expect mobility to be higher for relatively skilled workers, since language differences are not likely to be as much of a barrier for them as for their less skilled compatriots, and because migration costs will be tend to be smaller relative to any wage differential across countries.[24] In the host country, however, immigrants are generally expected to bid down wages and/or increase unemployment rates in the lower portion of the earnings distribution of the richer country, regardless of the fact that they would be regarded as relatively skilled in their native country. If the income of the owners of the mobile factors is also initially relatively high, then outward migration will increase the scarcity of a factor that is already well rewarded, driving up the return to that factor even more. Hence, the distribution of income will widen within the country of origin (although the *share* of national income going to that factor could either rise or fall). Furthermore, if the migrants compete with the unskilled rather than the skilled in the country of destination then the distribution of income will widen there too.

2.4 The lessons

These simple examples do not do justice to the extensive theoretical and empirical work on the distributional effects of trade and factor mobility. Much more complex and less predictable patterns are possible when more than two factors and two countries are involved, and the prediction that the incomes of factors that are abundant in autarky should be increased by integration can be tricky to flesh out empirically.[25]

Even when appropriately qualified, however, the lessons from these simple models about the distributional implications of economic integration are still of great relevance. Indeed if trade and factor mobility did not hurt at least some people, it would be hard to understand why trade liberalization and the removal of barriers to capital and labour mobility frequently encounter so much opposition. And, as we argue next, the idea that economic integration might be especially harmful to relatively poor individuals within rich countries has particularly insightful implications for the political economy of trade and social policies.

3 Social Policies in an International Context

'... I know which side my bread is buttered' said Jean-Pierre Meligon a self-employed electrician...'it has become impossible to run a small business in [France] because the charges are just too crippling'... M. Meligon, who pays, £7,000 a year to the French government in charges covering health insurance, pensions and family allowances is a would be tax exile with a difference... Like thousands of other French artisans and shopkeepers who have recently registered their businesses in Britain, he has no intention of leaving his native soil and setting up across the Channel... under a European directive... it is legal for the director of a company registered elsewhere in Europe – Britain for example – to pay his social charges there even if the business remains in France... the French government insists the practice is illegal and has condemned it as 'social dumping'... Martine Aubry, the employment minister, said... 'If you want to cut French hair or make baguettes and croissants for French people then you have to be installed in the French system'.

('Britain teaches us a lesson in liberté say French
firms crippled by taxes', *Daily Telegraph*, 17 April, 1998)

In this chapter we discuss how economic integration affects the demand for social protection, and how the presence of international interactions and spillovers affects the incentives for government to engage in such policies. In particular we try to highlight the circumstances in which coordination or harmonization might be desirable, and when it might not. First, however, we need to review the objectives and purposes of social policy.

3.1 What does social policy do?

Labour market regulations[26] and social policies more generally can serve two distinct purposes. First, they may counteract market failures, an example being unemployment insurance. If workers' inadequate access to credit markets prevents them from borrowing to sustain consumption in the face of job loss, then a mandatory state unemployment insurance scheme will allow the risks to be spread across the population. Participation needs to be mandatory to cope with the problem of 'adverse selection': if such a scheme were optional then workers with a very low risk of job loss would not find it worthwhile to participate in the scheme, and insurance providers would find that only those people who perceived themselves to be at major risk would sign up. A similar argument applies to health insurance.

A more subtle example is health and safety regulation. If the characteristics of a job are fully known to the work-force then it is not obvious why state regulation is required: workers in risky or unsafe environments would simply need to be duly compensated by receiving higher wages. Frequently, however, workers are not fully aware of the risks in the environment in which they work, and employers might well try to cut corners in order to boost their profits. In that case minimum standards could be enforced to overcome the information failure. Further information problems arise if the workers are covered by health insurance. The insurance providers are not likely to be well informed about conditions in the workplace. As a result workers need not bear the full economic consequences of their working conditions, which therefore will not be fully offset in higher wages. Similar arguments can also be applied to legislation on working hours, if excessive hours worked increase the likelihood of workplace accidents.

Social policy which is meant to redress market failures obviously increases economic efficiency, and on those grounds would be desirable. Regulations, however, can, and very often do, serve another purpose, namely redistributing income between different groups in society or protecting rents. While the imposition of a minimum wage can be justified on efficiency grounds as an attempt to curb the power of monopsonistic employers who can force down the conditions of employment below the level that would obtain in a competitive labour market, there is no doubt that for many workers it simply serves to redistribute income from the owners of (physical and human)[27] capital towards relatively unskilled labour. Similarly unemployment insurance, although addressing a market failure, also has the incidental effect of underpinning the level of wages (unless an availability-for-work test is vigorously enforced).

Where regulations seek mainly to redistribute income, they will tend to reduce, rather than increase, economic efficiency. Thus, labour standards and regulations frequently imply an effective decrease in the supply of labour.[28] This is most obviously true of prohibitions on child labour and mandatory reductions in working-time, both of which directly reduce the supply of labour. Unemployment insurance, however, has a similar effect by making the unemployed choosier about what jobs they will accept, and thus reduces both the effective supply of labour and the competitive pressures on the employed, resulting in higher wages and higher unemployment. Sometimes, however, the adverse effects on economic efficiency occur in a different way. For instance, employment security legislation slows both the rate at which labour is liberated from obsolete industries, and makes expanding firms reluctant to create new jobs unless they are confident that the expansion in demand will be maintained. The result is that labour is inefficiently allocated across the economy and the level of productivity is lowered.

In these circumstances there is a *trade-off* between economic efficiency and the level of social protection, in other words, between the average level of welfare and its distribution across society. Economic discussions of social policies and labour market regulation often focus narrowly on the first of these, ignoring the fact that the second is a legitimate social objective. In what follows we shall not discuss where societies should seek to locate on this frontier, which is a matter of social preference. Obviously, however, policies should be designed to *be* on that frontier. In reality governments do not necessarily act for the benefit of society as a whole, but rather to buy-off key interest groups or sections of the electorate, and as result socities may not be on that frontier. In this case, pressures to reduce regulations, or restructure them, so as to move the economy towards the frontier is desirable. Broadly speaking, then, we are: in favour of regulations that redress market failure; against regulations that protect rents and put the economy inside the efficiency-distribution frontier; and agnostic about changes in regulations that shift the economy along the frontier.

This discussion also draws attention to another fact, namely that we can expect those groups that benefit from regulation to try to stop it being removed. As a consequence, different people and groups within society will often have different perspectives on the desirability of (de)regulation, and this affects the political feasibility of reform. This needs to be borne in mind during our discussion of the interaction between economic integration and the implementation of social policy.

3.2 The demand for protection: integration and social policy

We saw in Chapter 2 that, absent other distortions, removing barriers to trade and factor mobility should benefit all individuals as consumers, but may well harm some of them in their role as producers. The same is true of the removal of other distortions to the market: monopolistic practices in the setting of prices or wages prevent economies from exhausting the potential gains from trade, but they equally clearly benefit businesses and workers respectively. A glib rejoinder to such distribution-motivated qualms about trade, factor mobility or competition in general, runs as follows. If markets functioned properly, there would be no reason for an individual's consumption to be tied to the income accruing to his or her specific bundle of factors: production should be organized efficiently, but people should then pool their resources so as to protect their consumption from movements in the incomes of different factors and occupations.

In practice such 'income-pooling' agreements are difficult, if not impossible, to draw up in respect of labour income (although they can be achieved in respect of capital income by holding a well-diversified portfolio). As a consequence, trade and factor mobility have adverse welfare implications for particular groups within society and will thus often encounter strong opposition: in political terms the pains from trade may well outweigh the gains. The attempt to deal with the distributional consequences of trade, competition and economic integration then offers a plausible explanation for the implementation of many distortionary policies.[29] Trade barriers and other limitations to economic integration, however much they may reduce economic efficiency, do redistribute income within a country, and may be preferable politically to other less distortionary, but more transparent, redistributive measures.

Once politics enters the picture, our discussion of how economic integration affects income distribution becomes relevant. Now much of the literature on the political economy of social policy and regulation focuses on policies that apply to, or favour, particular industries ('specific' policies); Box 3.1 notes that such 'specific' social policies are usually no more than disguised trade restrictions and we do not explore them further in this report. Instead we wish to focus on the interaction of across-the-board social policies ('general' policies) with economic integration. It has sometimes been argued – as exemplified in the Ohlin report – that such general policies will just lead to offsetting movements in wages and prices and are thus neutral in their effect. In that case there could not be any interesting interactions with economic integration. Box 3.1 argues that the view that general social policies are neutral is, however, mistaken. This is because general social policies still affect different people, and different parts of the economy, in very different ways.

Box 3.1 'Specific' and 'general' social policies

Standard approaches to the political economy of trade protection focus on the lobbying efforts of owners of *industry-specific* factors of production.[30] Some aspects of 'social' policy and regulation will bear on the competitiveness of particular industries. For example, exempting the tourist industry from strict job security provisions may well be justifiable because of the seasonal character of demand in tourism, but it certainly also reduces its costs. In other instances, detailed social provisions at the industry level can distort the pattern of production and trade in much the same way as do explicit tariffs. In the context of European integration, particular attention has been paid to the distinction between the distortions induced by 'general' and 'specific' policies in an attempt to isolate the industry-relevant aspects of social policy and regulation. This distinction was originally highlighted in the Ohlin report.[31]

Briefly, 'specific' social policy provisions are those that, by granting cost advantages to some, but not all, of the industries within a country, are essentially equivalent to the production or export subsidies called for by a mercantilist trade policy. Article 101 of the Treaty of Rome stipulates that national rules should not 'distort the conditions of competition', i.e. it forbids targeted social provisions which, like non-tariff barriers arising from national technical standards, primarily seek to distort the pattern of trade. Industry-level lobbying efforts may then concentrate on 'specific' aspects of social policy when, as in the EU, explicit trade protection and selective State aid are forbidden.

This focus on specific distortions has long led European treaties and institutions to neglect the more controversial interactions between economic integration and general social policy. This lacuna may be explained by the belief that general social policies were offset and thus neutral in their effect. Now, if only one type of undifferentiated labour were used in production, then economy-wide regulations would be equivalent to a reduction in the supply of labour, and could be expected to be offset by countervailing price, wage, and exchange rate adjustments. For example, taxes on labour income are higher in Germany than in Switzerland, and so is the provision of public services. What matters for employment and production, however, is the pre-tax wage, and to the extent that international differences in after-tax wages simply reflect differences in social provision there will be no impact on the pattern of trade and specialization. From this perspective, it then makes sense to view general social transfers and regulations as a matter of local policy with no international ramifications.

Such offsetting of general social policies is unlikely itself to be a general phenomenon, however. Indeed, general social policies would be pointless if offsetting was so complete as to make them neutral. In reality, of course, labour is not homogeneous, and more-over is not the only factor of production. Hence, regulations do not generally have the same effects on all factors and sectors even when they apply across the whole economy, and can be expected to have effects on production, trade and factor mobility.[32]

Thus, ignoring any other sources of comparative advantage, a country should tend to concentrate in industries that are relatively favoured by its chosen mode of regulation. For instance, heavily regulated labour markets favour large firms for whom an internal labour market offers a way round the obstacles to labour realloca-tion imposed by high firing costs and the like. Conversely, it discourages the self-employed and very small firms. It is, therefore, not surprising that Sweden, with a relatively high degree of social protection, is dominant in industries that tend to be characterised by larger firms.[33] By the same token, countries with 'rigid' labour markets will have a comparative advantage in the production of goods with relatively stable demand, while countries with flexible labour markets will have a comparative advantage in industries with volatile or unpredictable demand – which are often those pro-ducing the newest and most innovatory products – this might help

continued

continued from page 33
explain why innovation is so low in the EU compared to the US.[34]

As our discussion of the sharper, but qualitatively similar, issues arising in the context of North-South trade make clear, most social provisions will have distributional (and trade) effects even when they are imposed uniformly on all sectors, for the simple reason that not all sectors will be equally affected. The distinction between 'general' and 'specific' social provisions is useful as a first approximation, but is completely clear only in the rare case that within-country distributional aspects can be entirely neglected. Otherwise, 'general' social provisions will interact with economic integration.

Chapter 2 showed that economic integration can be expected to worsen the relative position of the unskilled workers in the richer countries. Expenditure on lobbying for protectionist measures may be lavish, but it tends to attract little political sympathy when it merely seeks to preserve the rents of a few. If both the price of a product and the incomes of those who make it are high, then it is relatively easy for politicians to see that increased competition would benefit consumers, and to endorse it. Thus, measures to increase competition in sectors with high barriers to entry in the EU, such as the Mutual Recognition of Professional Qualifications, clearly benefit consumers of professional services at the same time as they hurt a few rich producers, in other words, professionals in the countries with the most stringent barriers to entry. As we saw in Chapter 1, implementation of these measures may have proceeded disappointingly slowly, but this is more likely to reflect lobbying efforts, or genuine concerns about the comparability of qualifications, than democratic political pressures.

Things are different, however, when economic integration threatens the income of larger groups, especially if they are already relatively poor. The public may be indifferent to the income lost by a few dentists or lawyers as a result of increased competition among professionals, and they will certainly like the cheaper services that result. Whereas they will naturally be more sympathetic to the plight of poor native workers who lose their jobs in the face of low-cost foreign competition, or who are displaced by immigrants who are willing to work for lower wages. It is unsurprising that in such circumstances politicians may be less than enthusiastic about free trade and factor mobility. Of course, the workers from the poorer country would gain from the economic integration, but this may do little to reduce the sympathy for the losers in the rich country, because the gainers are strange immigrants and/or out-of-sight foreigners.

Attempts to prevent the adverse effects on the income distribution may then manifest itself in three ways: explicit or implicit trade barriers; policies to retard integration indirectly such as imposing social clauses on foreign countries or producers; and increased social protection at home. Box 3.2 discusses social clauses in the context of trade with less developed countries,[35] where even the most basic ILO standards are often not applied. The box shows that the first two policies are largely substitutes for each other, and in both cases it is the workers from the poor country who bear most of the burden.

Box 3.2 Social clauses, distribution and gains from trade

Eleven-year-old Imtyaz goes to school in the mornings and works in the afternoons in [Sialkot, Pakistan]'s thriving soccer ball industry. He is considered lucky. About 7,000 children between the ages of 5 and 14 have no time for school because they work full-time manufacturing soccer balls, earning about 50 cents for each ball they produce. As the World Cup approaches, bringing with it the spectre of bad publicity, the local industry has committed to putting a halt to its use of child labour over an 18-month period. It even wants international help to send the children to schools instead of into the factories. As the industry begins to clean up its act, big buyers like Nike, Reebok and Adidas have set up model factories that use adult-only workers. The workers also are paid slightly better – almost $2 a day... Many local people feel reform is doing more harm than good. They believe Western pressure may deprive local families of another source of income and drive children to other hazardous jobs. Observers say a better solution would be for factories to pay high enough wages to adult workers so that their children do not need to work.

('Pakistan soccer ball industry seeks end to child labour',
from CNN reporter Kasra Naji, 9 April 1998, Sialkot, Pakistan)

continued

continued from page 35

The terrible working conditions in less developed countries often prompt public opinion in the West to advocate banning imports of products from these countries unless Western standards are enforced, i.e. a *Social Clause* is included in trade agreements. The trade opportunities, however, largely derive from the willingness of the people of the poorer countries to work so hard for such low wages, so a legal requirement of good working conditions is tantamount to restricting trade and foregoing the gains from trade. And those gains accrue not only to consumers in the rich country, but also to workers in the poor country, at least to the extent that they voluntarily accept low-wage jobs in bad conditions. This might not be fully appreciated by Western public opinion, but it was certainly recognized by the local people of Sialkot when pressure was applied to end the use of child labour for stitching footballs.

Clearly, nothing in this argument denies that the unhappiness of poor workers in poor countries should be deplored. It does point, however, to the hypocrisy of the argument that the imposition of Western labour standards on poor countries is for their own good.[36] As noted in the text, the right comparison is between the same worker according to whether there is trade or not, not across different workers in more or less advantageous circumstances. If the poor voluntarily agree to work for low wages and in bad conditions then they will be made worse off if that is prevented.

Too often, then, the imposition of international labour standards simply amounts to implicit protectionism. Briefly, if stringent labour standards are applied across the board, production must fall. Welfare could improve if the standards happened to correctly reflect social values, but in that case the government of the poor country would have an incentive to introduce such standards on its own account. To adapt our whimsical example from earlier, suppose that for some reason British fashion designers and accountants were both required to wear gloves in the workplace. If such a dress code was privately optimal, say because workers were more productive when so clad, then Italians would also decide to wear them. If their climate or social customs let them do without gloves, however, would working barehanded grant them an 'unfair' advantage? The answer is No. An across-the-board standard in the UK will primarily change the pattern of absolute – not comparative – advantage, so no jobs will be destroyed and trade patterns will be unchanged with British workers simply consuming less in the way of physical goods but more welfare.

This, of course, is true only to a first approximation, for gloves may hamper shoe producers more or less than fashion designers; yet, stepping outside of our example and closer to EU facts and policies, this argument underlies the notion that 'general' social policies are not as harmful to the pattern of production and trade as 'specific' ones.[37] Moreover, even if the pattern of comparative advantage were to be somehow affected, it would not be 'unfair' for Italian workers to renounce a socially – if not privately – desirable standard, for in so doing they would only lower their own welfare at no obvious cost to British producers.

By contrast increased social protection for the affected groups at home involves redistribution from other domestic factors of production (typically redistributing income away from profits), which may create extra internal tensions. Thus, it is easy to see why politicians might prefer trade barriers or social clauses to enhanced social protection. Sometimes, however, the first will be impossible, e.g. because of World Trade Organization rules. In that case, increased social protection at home will be a political 'second-best'. Evidence that increased economic integration raises the demand for social protection is provided by the fact that social spending is not only higher in rich countries, which can better afford the luxury of protection, but also in countries, which are more open to international influences.[38]

In keeping with the evangelical command to 'Help thy neighbour', both social clauses and social protection help the *nearest* poor, if not the poorest in the world. In so doing, social clauses and social protection can, therefore, ensure that free trade and capital mobility do not generate excessive domestic political tensions, especially when tax competition and high government debt make it difficult to redistribute income through other channels. So, to the extent that the demand for more protection comes from, or is aimed at, the nearest poor it may be a reasonable response to the problem.

Too often, however, social policies are addressed neither at rectifying market failures, nor at protecting the incomes of the poorest members of society. Instead, 'social' policy has the effect of protecting particular – frequently comparatively well off – interest groups. A prime example is the high level of job security in many continental European economies, especially Spain. Originally intended to protect weak labourers against 'unfair' job loss, these high firing costs greatly reduce the probability of job loss for the employed 'insiders' in the labour market. Juxtaposed with fact that it is the insiders who are also most influential in setting wages, they simply ensure that those in work are insulated from competitive pressure from the unemployed 'outsiders', to the benefit of the former and the detriment of the latter. It is difficult to justify such policies on either distributional or efficiency grounds, although of course they make perfect sense to the insiders who can be expected to support them vigorously! This distinction between desirable and undesirable social policies has great relevance for whether coordination/harmonization or competition in the provision of social policies is appropriate.

3.3 The supply of protection

We have shown that economic integration, especially between unequal nations, is likely to raise the *demand* for social protection. Economic integration, however, also affects the *supply* of social protection. The reason is as follows: within a single country, regulations generally need to be imposed *erga omnes* if they are to be effective; otherwise they can be easily circumvented, nullifying their purpose. The same will then hold true in an integrated economy of many sovereign nations, as individual countries can seek to gain an advantage by adopting looser standards. The next sub-section explores this idea.

3.3.1 Spillovers and the 'race-to-the-bottom': the case for coordination

Economic integration adds an extra dimension to the implementation of social policies because the level of regulations in one country frequently has implications for other countries that are tied to it through product or factor markets. If policy-makers are indeed benevolent and social policies desirable (Section 3.3.2 discusses what happens if they are not), then uncoordinated policies will generally lead to sub-optimal levels of intervention or regulation. The resulting tensions may in turn prompt governments to try to obstruct the process of integration by pursuing (overt or subvert) protectionist policies against countries that they perceive as acting in an unsocial fashion – 'social dumping'. Agreement to coordinate or harmonize social policies then becomes a natural complement to economic integration.

As a canonical example of the importance of international coordination in social policy, consider the case of safety regulations and work rules aboard ships. It may or may not be desirable to impose such rules, but if it is, then their efficacy is clearly hampered by lack of international coordination: it is only too easy for shipping companies to escape regulations by incorporating and registering their vessels in more lenient jurisdictions, such as Panama and Liberia. By contrast, regulations can be enforced more easily in the non-tradable sector, so it may no coincidence that the service sector is so heavily regulated and underdeveloped in European countries relative to the US.[39] Even in the service sector the issue can arise, however, as the case of Jean-Pierre Meligon, quoted at the beginning of this chapter, attests.

The most obvious example of such spillovers in the choice of social policy lies in the field of social spending. Spending on things like education and health, as well as on unemployment benefits and social security presently varies greatly across the members of the EU. On the, admittedly unrealistic, assumption that governments aim to maximize some notion of social welfare, a government in a closed economy deciding how much to tax and spend would have to weigh the desirability of increased levels of spending on these items against the costs of having to impose a higher tax burden on the electorate: optimality requires that the marginal social return from an extra unit of spending is equal to the marginal social cost of financing it through higher taxes.

Consider, however, what happens when the economy is open to trade in goods and some factors of production – say, capital – are internationally mobile. Acting alone a government will be tempted to implement a more advantageous tax regime on capital so as to encourage an inward flow of capital. If capital mobility is high and sensitive to international differences in tax rates, then the inward flow of capital can be large for even a small cut in tax rates. This inflow of capital will tend to drive up wages and, even if taxes have been increased on labour (the immobile factor) to compensate for the reduction in taxes on capital, the result may be an increase in wages net of tax. Indeed, it is even possible that taxes on labour could fall if the proportionate increase in the size of the capital tax base out-weighs the proportionate reduction in the tax rate on capital! The flip side of this is, however, that the size of the tax base in *other* countries contracts, necessitating either higher tax rates on the immobile factors there or lower public spending – a negative 'fiscal externality'.

This assumes, however, that the tax regimes of other countries are unchanged. This is unlikely to happen, and all countries will be tempted to engage in a 'beggar-my-neighbour' game of bidding down the tax rate on capital – a 'race-to-the-bottom'. As the elasticity of supply of capital to all countries together will be considerably lower than to any one individual country on its own, the result will be an inefficiently low level of taxes on capital, and an excessively high level of taxes on labour, or alternatively a much reduced supply of public goods and transfers. An agreement to coordinate tax rates on mobile factors, and in particular to prevent them being pushed ever downwards, will then produce a better outcome. In this environment subsidiarity is bad, and coordination good.

These considerations do not just apply to physical capital, but also to the owners of human capital as these workers are typically – although not always – more internationally mobile than unskilled workers. One obvious response to the distributional strains imposed on the developed countries by globalization and skill-biased technical change, both of which reduce the demand for unskilled labour, is to increase the progressivity of the tax system. If high earners can, how-ever, easily relocate to pleasant tax havens (such as Switzerland), such a policy may be of only limited effectiveness. Thus, not only does integration tend to directly hurt the poor in rich countries through depressing their wages, it may also hurt them indirectly by increasing their share of the tax burden (assuming they are not very mobile).

As another example of the need to coordinate social policies consider working-time reduction. Historically, legal restrictions on working hours were seen as a way of protecting workers from unscrupulous monopsonistic employers, their effect being to produce a general reduction in labour supply. Current French law aims to reduce the standard work-week further to 35 hours by the early years of the next millennium, and the Italian government is sponsoring similar legislation under pressure from the Communist Refoundation Party.[40] The effects of this action will be limited if unit labour costs are unaffected; in that case output will simply be lower and the consumption of leisure higher (or, in the case of work sharing, output may be unchanged and leisure distributed differently). The opposition of business organizations to a mandated (rather than negotiated) shorter work-week indicates that such legislation is expected to increase production costs, rather than simply facilitate work sharing (or, equivalently, unemployment sharing). The effect of these higher costs then depends critically on how easily substitutable are the more expensive goods and labour: if substitutability is high then the efficacy of the policy will be greatly reduced. If production can be relocated to unregulated labour markets then, as in the case of other labour market regulations aimed at improving the lot of workers, substitution by foreign workers would defeat the purpose of the regulation. For the 35-hour legislation to be effective it would then need to be imposed across the board in as many competing sectors as possible, and in as many countries as possible.

Recognition of this interaction between integration and the supply of social policy is not a new phenomenon. Sometimes foreign competition has been used as a justification against social measures: Jacques Necker, Finance Minister to Louis XVI, invoked international competition as an argument against abolishing Sunday work in France. At other times, the successful enactment of social policy has required coordination to prevent it being undermined by 'unfair' competition: in 1818 Robert Owen, the grandfather of British labour law, petitioned the Powers for continent-wide regulation of working hours so as to achieve 'fair' competition.[41] Such concerns are likely to be to the fore in the next few years as the process of deepening European integration proceeds apace, and the EU expands to embrace the countries of Central and Eastern Europe with their significantly lower wage costs and very different institutional structures.

A natural question is why all this is any different from competition between countries based on wage differences. Indeed, workers in manufacturing industries in developed countries suddenly exposed to competition from low wage producers in developing countries often *do* claim that such competition is unfair – witness television broadcasts of redundant US auto-production workers taking axes to Toyotas and Nissans during the 1980s when the dollar was so high. We usually recognize that in reality this is often simply special pleading for the protection of rents or for compensation in the face of economic development. The issue is, however, subtly different here:

whereas wages are largely the outcome of the interplay of the impersonal forces of supply and demand in labour and product markets, in the case of taxation, spending and social policies these are set by governments, and can be set strategically so as to influence the outcome in favour of themselves. Trying to categorize such regulatory competition as 'fair' or 'unfair' is frankly not particularly helpful; but what we should be able to agree is that, as long as the policies under consideration are those that a benevolent central planner would favour, such competition leads to an inferior outcome compared to that which would obtain under coordination.

3.3.2 *Cuius regio, eius religio* and competition between rules: the case for diversity

Our analysis so far suggests that coordination in the implementation of social policies and regulatory frameworks is necessary in order to prevent individual countries implementing laxer regimes which are intended to create a competitive advantage and attract inward migration of mobile factors of production, especially capital. In a nutshell, rules and regulations need to be implemented in a coordinated way if they are to serve their intended purpose, *whether or not those policies are themselves desirable*. Thus, it might appear difficult to subscribe to the view that competition in the choice of policies is efficient, except in the special case where general social policies are fully offset and, therefore, neutral (which as we argued earlier is any case generally not so). Nevertheless, there are valid arguments for competition and diversity in social policies and regulatory frameworks.

First, coordination is not the same as harmonization. The demand for social protection tends to increase as countries grow richer,[42] and it would make no sense to enforce identical standards across countries at different levels of development. It is entirely rational that workers in less developed countries are willing to work for lower wages, and in worse conditions, than their counterparts in developed countries. The resulting national differences are then the basis for comparative advantage and mutually beneficial gains from trade, with the less developed countries specializing in the production of labour-intensive goods and the developed countries specializing in production of (physical and human) capital-intensive goods. Of course, as we saw above, there may be adverse effects on unskilled workers in the developed country – the 'nearest poor'. Insisting, however, that workers in the less developed country be subject to the *same* standards and – even worse – wages as those in the more developed country erases the advantages of trade, is inherently protectionist, and harms rather helps the workers in the less developed country. As Box 3.2 on p. 35 indicates the morality of this is distinctly dubious.

This is not to deny that some level of regulation will be appropriate in less developed countries, for the reasons discussed at the start of this chapter. Asymmetric information between workers and firm owners makes legislation on health and safety standards appropriate; incomplete credit and insurance markets make unemployment and health insurance appropriate; and the presence of unscrupulous monopsonistic employers makes limitations on child work appropriate. There is simply no reason at all, however, why the appropriate *level* of regulation should be the same in all countries. All that subsection 3.3.1 establishes is that the consequences of a given set of policies for both efficiency and distribution need to be evaluated taking into account spillovers across jurisdictions.

Furthermore, even for countries of similar levels of development, there is no reason for them to share exactly the same tastes for regulation, which often may stem from differences in social philosophies. To take but one obvious example, the US has shown a preference for generally lower levels of regulation and social protection than the European countries. Arguably this has helped it to achieve a better unemployment record in recent years, but the flip side has been that the distribution of income has worsened markedly in a way that has not generally happened in Europe, with a resulting worsening in social tension between the haves and the have-nots. This is not to deny that some reform of European labour markets is required to reduce the current horrendous levels of unemployment,[43] merely to reinforce the point that there is a trade-off between economic efficiency and social protection, and that different societies may come to a different political consensus as to where along this trade-off they wish to be. There is no reason even to expect economic integration and income convergence across nations to lead to a political consensus on appropriate standards.

Effective coordination of *different* policies and regulatory environments is, however, something that is difficult to achieve, as a national government would always have an incentive to dissemble, saying that lighter regulations were appropriate for reasons of domestic tastes, while in reality seeking to gain an advantage thereby. In that case, harmonization and uniformity may be the only practical option, in which case the need to accommodate diversity in incomes and tastes dictates that harmonization should take the form of *minimum* standards, leaving countries free to adopt stricter regulations if they wish (and recognizing that race-to-the-bottom pressures could push these below desirable levels).

All this points to the presumption that *extensive harmonization of standards will be more likely to be appropriate between countries at a similar standard of development.* This is of particular relevance to future enlargement of the EU, as the gap between living standards in many of the aspiring entrants and the more wealthy members of the EU is two to three times greater than the gap between the *per capita* incomes of the rich and poor countries of the present EU. While 'help-my-neighbour' political pressures can understandably generate calls for extensive harmonization across countries at very different stages of development, agreement on viable minimum standards is all that policy-makers should seek to achieve.

There is, however, a second, and more subtle, argument as to why competition among social policies, rather than coordination/harmonization might be desirable. While ensuring the effectiveness of social policies in an integrated economy requires international coordination, whether or not those policies are themselves desirable, in arguing for coordination/harmonization we were implicitly assuming that these policies were desirable, either to counteract market failures or as a second-best distributional policy to help the (nearest) poor. We noted, however, at the start of this chapter that social policies sometimes protect the rents of the not-so-poor, or are simply inefficient in achieving their ends. When social policies are undesirable, or undesirably restrictive, and regulatory failure is pervasive, then competition between different (national or local) jurisdictions rules will put pressure on legislators to adopt better and more efficient policies.[44] In this case, then, any race-to-the-bottom should be seen as good, rather than bad. This leads us to a second presumption, namely that *coordination/harmonization is desirable when the policies themselves are desirable, and undesirable when the policies themselves are undesirable.*

We should also briefly note a third argument in favour of permitting diversity in social and regulatory policies. Our knowledge of the exact impact of policies is often uncertain, and policies often turn

out to have unintended consequences. In these circumstances, allowing countries to follow different policies permits countries to learn
from the experience of others what works and what does not.

These positive aspects to regulatory competition are in our view
particularly relevant to many aspects of continental European social
policy in general, and labour markets in particular. Originally meant
to protect the poor, they are now entangled in a web of specific provisions that simply boost the income of insiders to the detriment of
the disadvantaged. From our own perspective, then, the pressure for
change that comes with integration is generally to be welcomed.

We should conclude by noting that even if social protection is too
high, it will not be *unanimously* perceived to be too high, for some
groups (if only union leaders and regulators) will gain from high
levels of regulations and transfers. The political stability of the current system suggests that the outsiders who suffer as a consequence
of the high levels of social protection are either too few to carry political clout, or else strongly linked (via family) to the insiders who gain
by the rigidity. Consequently, even where social policy is badly
designed or harmful, we should recognize that reform will be painful
for some groups and therefore difficult to implement, while the privileged groups will resist both genuine integration and deregulation.

<u>3.4</u> Social protection: the balance of demand and supply

We have seen that social policy and economic integration inevitably
interact. Since income distribution *within* countries is generally
affected by opportunities for trade and cross-border factor mobility,
those who suffer are likely to seek compensation: when the losers are
many and relatively poor – as is likely to be the case within rich
countries – the relevant compensation may win political support and
take the form of protection through 'social policy'. As we have seen,
however, economic integration affects the supply of protection as
well as the demand for it: the redistribution of income or welfare is
not easy to accomplish and can become impossible when people and
businesses can escape taxation by moving to other jurisdictions.

Throughout much of the post-war period, income levels, economic integration and social spending have grown apace, both in
Europe and in the global economy. Indeed, there is no clear evidence
of race-to-the-bottom trends even in the taxation of very mobile fac-

tors such as capital which might seem to suggest these forces are unimportant.[45] From our perspective, however, this suggests that historically the determination of social policy provision has been dominated by the trends in demand, rather than in supply. It certainly does not refute the hypothesis that, in the absence of coordination, supplying a high level of social protection is more problematic in more integrated economies. Here, we elaborate on this basic point and explore some examples to illustrate the role of supply factors in determining the real-life extent and character of social protection.

We have already noted that the relatively low provision of social protection in the US may simply reflect American tastes. Still, the similarity of US and European income levels at least suggests the US provides a natural benchmark for evaluating the potential significance of tax competition[46] and a race-to-the-bottom in an integrated Europe. After all, both capital and labour are even more mobile in the US than is likely in an integrated Europe, so one would certainly expect tax competition to be even more important there. Indeed, the structure of US Federal and State budgets does suggest that institutional structure and jurisdictional competition play an important role in the supply of social provision.

In the US, as well as the Federal income tax, there are also State and local income taxes, which do vary, although invariably there are some jurisdictions with taxes set at very low levels. In respect of sales taxes, there is no Federal value added or sales tax, but there are State sales taxes, whose rates again vary, ranging from zero to around 8%.[47] At first glance this appears to imply that competition will *not* necessarily force all tax rates down to the lowest common denominator. This is not the right conclusion, however. What we *do* learn from the US experience is that without explicit harmonization at the Federal/supra-national level, differences in tax rates can persist if there are *other* reasons why people might prefer to live and work in one locality than another – a sort of 'compensating differential'. For instance, some people might like to live and work in New York even though the taxes are high there, because they like the buzz of a big city or need face-to-face contact with Wall Street colleagues. The race-to-the-bottom then implies not that *all* tax rates are pushed to zero, but rather the *low* tax locations are characterized by zero tax rates, and correspondingly low levels of public goods provision and social expenditure.

While we illustrated the key role of coordination in the context of tax and social spending policy, similar forces are at work in the context of workplace regulation, pensions, unemployment benefits and minimum wage, and indeed the whole gamut of social policies. Take for instance, health and safety regulation and other workplace regulations, these raise the effective cost of labour and reduce profitability and discourage investment. An obvious way for a government to encourage foreign direct investment (FDI) into the country is, therefore, to offer a lightly regulated working environment. If countries compete along this dimension then the result will be a race-to-the-bottom in terms of labour standards, rather than in capital taxes.

The consequences of a lack of coordination in social policies can also be illustrated with reference to the US. Other than safety net arrangements like Medicaid, there is no system of national health insurance, and the States have not sought to introduce their own, possibly reflecting race-to-the-bottom pressures. Instead, most health insurance is private, tailored to the known characteristics of the insured, and frequently paid for by the employer as part of the worker's overall compensation package. There is, however, no coordinated portability of coverage across insurers, so if a worker, or a dependent, develops a health condition then the resulting premiums if he or she moves to another provider will be higher (or benefits lower), thus discouraging workers from changing employer or occupation (a phenomenon known as 'job lock'[48]).

The US also offers an interesting reference point with respect to unemployment insurance. This is set at the State level, benefits are not particularly generous, and usually payable for only a short period. As a result, their impact on the location of the work-force is pretty small. More generally, in 1969 the US Supreme Court decided that States could *not* make welfare benefits contingent on residence-to-date, thus making 'social tourism' a real possibility. This obviously makes it more difficult for individual States to be generous as they are likely to become 'welfare magnets'. What then saves the US from a race-to-the-bottom in terms of the provision of social spending is the fact that much of the social expenditure is Federal (Supplemental Social Security, Food Stamps, Earned Income Tax Credit, etc.) or else involves matching Federal grants (Medicaid).[49] The EU, by contrast, does not at present have any such supra-national scheme of social support. Furthermore, concerns in countries such as Germany about even the present levels of payments into the EU budget make the development of any such scheme in the near future distinctly unlikely.

To illustrate the potential relevance of race-to-the-bottom tendencies in the European context, Box 3.3 discusses a telling example drawn from recent German experience. The employment and profit opportunities of German construction workers and firms were not boosted by the exceptional construction activity in the former East German regions after unification, because under the Single Market programme they were open to competition from construction firms based in other countries. Clearly, this competition was good on efficiency grounds. Since the foreign workers were willing to accept lower wages and worse working conditions (away from home!) than German construction workers, the German government and other purchasers were able to obtain construction services at a lower price from these foreign firms. The episode featured a 'social dumping' dimension, however, because the German safety net protected German workers from bearing the full brunt of foreign competition, by granting them unemployment benefits (and particularly generous ones at that, designed to offer protection against the cyclical and seasonal job loss that characterizes the construction industry). Consequently, the transfer of resources from the German taxpayer to unemployed German construction workers was larger in the integrated European economy than it would have been if foreigners had not been available to underbid German wage demands: economic integration increased the demand for protection, but also made it more expensive to supply.

The most interesting aspect of the posted workers case study is its resolution. By imposing a minimum wage law on foreign workers posted to work in Germany and simultaneously reducing unemployment benefits for German construction workers, the German government aimed to shift some of the welfare burden away from the German taxpayer. In so doing the gains from economic integration were reduced (construction projects became more expensive) as was the degree of social protection offered to the German unemployed construction workers (more of whom should thus become available for work as a result of the reduction in unemployment benefits).

The posted worker tale is probably not that important itself on a European, or even a German, scale; there were 315,000 posted workers in 1990 (around 0.4% of EU employees), increasing to 554,000 in 1994 (0.6% of employees). It does illustrate, however, many of the issues that arise in the debate on the Social Clause and social dumping: just as Western footballers gain from the willingness of Pakistani

Box 3.3 **Posted workers: a case study in economic integration and social policy**

Yesterday, the Bundestag approved a law reducing subsidies to the long-term unemployed. Simultaneously, the Bundesrat legislated restrictive rules for the employment of workers from other European countries on German construction sites. ... the reduction of unemployment subsidies aims at savings of over DM 2 billion a year... while imposition of German minimum wage standards represents a protectionist move to limit substitution of foreign workers for the 150,000 German construction workers who are currently unemployed. [The minimum-wage and mandatory holiday provisions] face opposition by the three employer confederations; only construction firms are favourable, as they see an opportunity to restore their competitiveness against foreign firms employing Portuguese and British workers. ... ANCE, the Italian confederation of construction firms, attempts to rescue firms engaged in German construction projects. A protectionist stance is explicitly blamed on German authorities ... a delegation will leave to Germany tomorrow to explore how tensions between local commitments and Italian firms may be eased.

(Translated from 'Colpiti i lavoratori a casa da oltre un anno/ Intervento per i salari nell'edilizia/Bonn: da aprile sussidi piu' bassi per molti lavoratori tedeschi', *Il Sole 24 Ore*, 10 February, 1996; and 'Le norme in arrivo sui salari penalizzano le imprese edili italiane', *Il Sole 24 Ore*, 13 February, 1996.)

On 1 March, 1996, a minimum wage of DM18 per hour was introduced for all construction work performed in Germany; this minimum wage applied irrespective of both the worker's nationality and the country where his or her employment contract was drafted and signed. The relevant piece of legislation was passed almost simultaneously with another that substantially reduced the unemployment benefits payable in the construction sector. The two laws were quite transparently related, and motivated by the peculiar situation that saw increasing unemployment among German construction workers at the same time as East German reconstruction proceeded at the hands of a veritable army of foreign workers operating under contracts won by British, Portuguese and Italian

continued

continued from page 49

construction firms (under Single Market rules that require public procurement contracts to be open to competitive tendering).

Out of about 1.3 million German construction workers, roughly 400,000 were unemployed in early 1997, and about the same number of foreign workers were legally or illegally employed on German construction sites. In Berlin alone, alongside 40,000 German workers, there were 30,000 workers from other EU countries, some 8,000 legal East Europeans, and an estimated 25,000 illegal workers; but there were also about 17,000 unemployed German construction workers. The hourly wage of foreign workers, in the neighbourhood of DM14 before the minimum wage law became binding, were lower even than the generous, and essentially open-ended, unemployment benefits of German unemployed construction workers.

German construction businesses, but not employers at large, were in favour of the minimum wage law. Not surprisingly, a heated debate ensued in Brussels and Strasbourg as foreign construction firms and governments contested the validity of the legislation. Eventually, the European Commission issued the Posted Workers Directive (96/71/EC) which, while restating the principle of free labour mobility in the Single Market, admitted that this and similar national legislation was legal. This Directive is very carefully phrased and purports to protect freedom of service provision and fair competition; to justify the imposition of minimum compensation standards, the Directive invokes 'Social Clause' arguments, purporting to prevent 'exploitation' of guest workers.

children to work for low wages (see Box 3.2 on p. 35), German purchasers of construction projects gained through the lower wages paid to posted workers. In both cases, gains from trade are belied by more or less explicit social concerns, and charges of 'social dumping' result from distributional tensions working their way through to government budgets strained by international fiscal spillovers. The next two chapters bring these ideas to bear on more generally on economic integration within Western and with Eastern countries, where the same issues are likely to reappear on a much bigger – if qualitatively similar – scale.

4 Lessons from the Past: Trade, Foreign Direct Investment and Enlargements

As detailed negotiations about expanding the European Union get going, which western country could be better placed to hold the EU presidency than Austria? It borders – and used to rule – three of the five front-runners: Hungary, Slovenia and the Czech Republic. It once ruled the southern chunk of a fourth, Poland, with which it has strong historical ties. ... But as Austrian politicians preen themselves for six months in the limelight, starting in July, their public is grumpier. Most Austrians, polls say, doubt the wisdom of the EU's eastward expansion. They fear crime and competition as easterners come offering cheap and easy labour. One Austrian politician has warned that 200,000 of them would migrate into his region every year if the EU expanded unchecked.

('Austria and its eastern neighbours', The Economist, May 9 1998, p. 35.)

In the previous two chapters we found it useful to illustrate general theoretical interactions between economic integration and social policy provision with references to North-South trade and to the character of social policies in the US. The 'Posted Workers' experience reviewed at the end of Chapter 3 indicates that qualitatively similar issues are indeed relevant in the European context. In this chapter we assess broader interactions between economic integration and social policy in EU experience. We first review the scope for 'social dumping' and 'race-to-the-bottom' tensions arising from factor mobility, focusing in particular on the highly visible capital flows associated with foreign direct investment decisions. We then go on to look at previous enlargements of the EU to see what can be learnt about the effects of integration and social policy. We conclude by addressing the prospect of future enlargement to include the formerly Communist Central and Eastern Europe Countries (CEECs).

4.1 Foreign direct investment and the scope for social dumping

In the light of our previous analysis, foreign direct investment (FDI) decisions are a particularly important source of such interactions. If FDI is sensitive to labour costs and taxes, then there will be scope for 'social dumping' through the strategic choice of social policies and regulatory regimes.

We have seen that the various EU countries have very different social policies, in respect of both labour market regulations and social protection. These and other differences in labour market structure (e.g. in collective bargaining systems), as well as in income and wealth levels, make for very different labour costs across the EU and thus might be expected to affect the location of production. In 1994, hourly labour costs in industry in West Germany were 54% higher than the average of the EU12, while in Portugal they were 67% lower. Moreover, these figures are not much different from ten years earlier, when they were 41% and 76% respectively. A synthetic measure of the divergence in labour costs across countries indicates a drop of just 7% over the period (see Table 4.1).

On the one hand, these figures do overstate the cross-country disparity in production costs, because productivity also tends to be higher in those countries with higher labour costs. In other words, there is far less difference in unit labour costs. Nevertheless, firms can easily take their production methods abroad, assuming that the labour force there is suitably skilled, and may achieve higher productivity than that prevailing on average in the host country. Furthermore, the data in Table 4.1 will understate the incentives for FDI to the extent that they refer to whole countries. For example, a German firm considering opening a plant in another country would look at the labour costs in the different regions of the country it was contemplating moving to, and we know that the within-country disparity in labour costs is also quite large. Thus, if we go just to the NUTS1 level of regional disaggregation, in 1992 we find the lowest hourly industrial wage costs to be around 5 ECU in parts of Portugal and 7 ECU in parts of Greece. At the other extreme, hourly costs were 23–4 ECU in Paris and most of West Germany, and as high as 27 ECU in Hamburg.[50] This variation is significantly higher than that across US States (which roughly corresponds to the NUTS1 level of disaggregation), where hourly labour costs ranged from $14 in Mississippi,

Table 4.1 Hourly labour costs in industry in the EU

	1984	*1988*	*1992*	*1994*
Belgium	132.9	136.4	133.3	142.9
Denmark	118.5	124.7	120.8	124.1
France	122.7	122.7	119.8	121.3
West Germany	141.2	146.9	145.0	154.0
Germany			75.0	96.8
Greece	58.0	43.0	43.7	45.0
Ireland	88.7	85.4	80.2	77.9
Italy	106.4	114.5	117.4	99.4
Luxembourg	109.8	109.4	107.5	113.1
Netherlands	135.7	131.6	120.7	125.6
Portugal	23.6	24.0	34.8	32.5
Spain	73.0	73.4	94.7	83.2
United Kingdom	89.6	88.2	82.1	81.0
EU12 (1990)[1]	100.0	100.0	100.0	100.0
Austria	109.0	118.6	124.4	134.1
Finland			110.0	105.0
Sweden	117.9	116.0	119.2	94.5
Divergence[2]	**48.2**	**51.6**	**42.6**	**44.9**

[1] EU12 (1990) refers to the old territorial situation of the EU with 12 member states, and without the new German Länder. It is an unweighted average.
[2] Divergence: standard deviation of the logarithms of the labour costs.
Sources: Eurostat, *Labour Cost Survey*, 1997. For Spain in 1984, *Year Book of Labour Statistics*, International Labour Organisation, 1994.

South Dakota and Arkansas, up to \$20 in Ohio and Washington and a high of \$23 in Michigan. From these numbers we may conclude that there are large enough differences in labour costs across the EU to warrant both movements in goods (trade) and capital (FDI). Also, regarding labour regulations, informal and formal evidence for the 1980s and 1990s suggests that for given labour costs, net FDI inflow is unsurprisingly related inversely to the stringency of labour regulations.[51] The empirical evidence does not, however, suggest that labour costs in general, or labour regulations in particular, are the paramount determinant of either trade or FDI within the EU. Let us take each in turn.

Differences in labour costs are most relevant if trade flows are driven by basic comparative advantage as described in Chapter 2. As mentioned there, trade flows may also be the consequence of firms' ability to reap economies of scale by clustering together, drawing on specialized workers and suppliers, and benefiting from knowledge spillovers.[52] This motivation for trade tends to be associated with trade in similar, rather than dissimilar, products, so its empirical relevance is indicated by the volume of trade taking place within industries, rather than between them. 'Two-way' trade in similar goods (intra-industry trade) represents the majority of intra-EU trade – some 63% in 1994.[53] The remaining 37% represents 'one-way' trade in dissimilar goods (inter-industry trade), and thus provides a rough indication of the relative importance of labour costs as determinants of trade. By the same token, it reveals that the scope for 'social dumping' based on lower labour costs and less stringent labour regulations is limited within the EU. Moreover, it is revealing that the two countries in which inter-industry trade, as a share of their total trade with the rest of the EU, fell the most from 1987 to 1994 are two of the poorest EU countries, Spain (–12%) and Portugal (–9%). We will return to the case of these countries below.

Among FDI activities, plant relocations are more visible than other adjustments, and hence tend to excite more resentment. For example, in January 1993 Hoover Europe, a US-owned company, closed a vacuum cleaner plant with 700 employees in Burgundy in France and relocated production to an existing site in Scotland, as a result of the Scottish plant's unions agreeing to various labour conditions (limited contract work, no pension rights for the first two years, highly flexible working times, etc.) inferior to those prevailing at the French factory.[54] Both the media and politicians took this as a prime case of social dumping in the Single Market. France and the UK were on the different sides of the fence in regard to social policy harmonization. The preceding year the UK had refused to sign the Agreement on Social Policy and, moreover, the pound had depreciated by around 20% since it had left the exchange rate mechanism of the European Monetary System. In such cases, however, there are also bound to be firm-specific circumstances. Without considering them it would be hard to understand, for example, why around the same time Nestlé Rowntree decided that it would transfer some of its activities from Scotland to Burgundy. And labour regulations can cut both ways. For instance, the average redundancy pay per worker paid by Thomson when it closed its television plant in Gosport (UK) was but one-seventh of that in Spain.

Whatever its cause, EU social policy could not have prevented Hoover's decision to relocate. Only the coordination of workers' representatives at its plants in different countries might have prevented the decision, fostered by the recent Social Chapter directive on European works councils mentioned earlier. The increasingly multinational character of companies gives management increased bargaining power *vis-à-vis* their employees in any one plant or country by allowing them to threaten a switch of production to a more favourable outside alternative. The directive can be regarded as providing workers with a vehicle for coordination to countervail such increased bargaining power.

FDI has indeed grown phenomenally in the last two decades. Over the period 1981–90 cumulative FDI outflows from OECD countries amounted to 1,027 billion dollars and inflows to these countries amounted to 850 billion dollars, some 3.4 and 4.5 times the amounts in 1971–80, respectively. The EU shares of these flows was 55% and 42% respectively, with the more backward countries of the EU – the four recipients of Cohesion Fund monies (Greece, Ireland, Portugal and Spain) – attracting no less than 17% of the inflows into the EU.[55]

That labour costs are not the only determinant of FDI, is attested by the fact that FDI flows from developed to developing countries are much smaller than those between developed ones.[56] Firms may indeed engage in FDI activity, rather than export to a given market, to take advantage of locational advantages, like cheaper factors of production. Other advantages of this type are, however, also very relevant, like gaining easier access to consumers or avoiding barriers to trade, either natural ones, such as transportation costs, or policy imposed ones, such as tariffs or quotas.[57] Moreover, FDI can also be caused by multinational companies having ownership-specific advantages (e.g. its production process or brand name) or the chance to exploit internalization advantages making it more profitable to set up their own foreign subsidiaries rather than, for example, license their products to other firms. Lastly, FDI may be prompted by economies of scale, either at the firm or plant levels, as in the case of intra-industry trade.[58]

Both raw data and more formal empirical work support the thesis that labour costs are not the only, or even the most important, determinant of FDI.[59] For example, over the period 1990–3, while Ireland stands out with total FDI amounting to 9.4% of its GDP, both Belgium-Luxembourg, with 4.7%, and the Netherlands, with 2.7%, receive more FDI than Portugal, at 2.4%, and Spain, at 1.8%. Indeed, Greece, with FDI equal to 0.4% of its GDP, shows the lowest inflow in the EU. Moreover, FDI into service industries, which is not likely to be moving in search of cheap labour, represented 63% of cumulative FDI inflows to the EU from 1984 to 1993, with manufacturing industries receiving only 31%.[60] We therefore conclude that, despite the view of both politicians and laymen, labour cost differences across the EU have not been their most important determinant of trade and FDI in this integrated European economy.

Both the public and policy-makers believe that taxes have a strong effect on FDI: witness the strong resistance encountered by recent attempts to establish an off-shore processing centre in Trieste, and discussions of Irish tax incentives to FDI. The empirical effect of taxes on FDI is, however, somewhat elusive. The European Commission's Single Market review exercise[61] focuses on non-tax factors as determinants of FDI flows. Only in Appendix B.6.2 of that review are tax issues addressed, with reference to qualitative survey evidence that nearly half of production location decisions are affected to some extent by tax considerations. As to quantitative evidence, the Single Market review exercise offers only a half-hearted attempt at including relative corporate tax rates in models of aggregate UK and German FDI flows. In the preferred specification the tax variables are insignificant and incorrectly signed, but this may simply tell us about the difficulty of trying to detect such potentially complex effects with aggregate data. More convincing is microeconometric evidence for a panel of US firms which conclusively rejects the notion that taxes do not matter; that study finds that each percentage point of tax-induced variation in the user cost of capital has a 1–2 percentage point impact on the investment rate.

4.2 Past enlargements

Our analysis in earlier chapters has pointed to the fact that the tensions that lead to charges of social dumping are more likely to occur when economies that are very different in structure, factor endowments or income levels are integrated, for in these cases the distributional effects are more likely to be significant and the political pressure for countervailing measures more intense. The past enlargement of the EU from its original six members, in particular to incorporate the four poorer countries that currently receive monies from the Cohesion Funds (Greece, Ireland, Portugal and Spain, in 1981, 1973, 1986 and 1986 respectively), is therefore likely to be instructive.

Trade patterns between incumbent and newer members of the EU do indicate that the Cohesion Fund countries were not only poorer, but also quite different in the structural aspects that are most relevant to our arguments. In 1987, among the original six members of the European Community, two-way trade in similar products ranged between 10.4% (Italy) and 21.6% (Belgium-Luxembourg) of intra-EU12 trade; the UK also fell within this range at 18.4%. As pointed out in Chapter 2, such 'intra-industry' trade is unlikely to have distributional implications of the type we focus on in this report. In the same year, however, only 2.9% of intra-EU trade by Greece was two-way in similar products, and even Ireland at 8.8% was lagging well behind the core members of the EU.[63] By 1994 the highest ratio was reached by France, at 24.1%, while Greece still lagged at just 3.7%. Hence, trade and actual or potential factor mobility across the borders of late-accession countries are likely motivated by classic technological or factor-endowment differences. Theory leads us to expect recent stages of European integration to have potentially adverse distributional effects on relatively poor producers within rich countries and important social policy repercussions.

In Chapter 1 we noted that in the mid-1980s the Single Market programme coincided with the enlargement of the EU to include countries which were significantly poorer than the average 10 incumbents. At the official level, the outcome was two-faced, with both increased pressure for pan-European social policy and income transfers towards poor regions through the Cohesion Funds. The Treaty of Rome already recognized that harmonization of social policies are only one side of the coin, the other one being redistributive policies as carried out by the European Social Fund (and later by the Common Agricultural Policy), but the doubling of the Structural Funds so as to accommodate the new members represented a watershed. It is not hard to understand why it happened, though. From the point of view of the incumbents, the potentially adverse effects of integration on their less skilled workers would be mitigated if the Cohesion Funds could help raise living standards (and labour costs) in the new entrants; they might also reduce the incentives for immigration from those countries. From the point of view of the newcomers, the potential loss of competitiveness caused by the increase in their labour costs arising from the adoption of the *acquis communautaire*, social and otherwise, would be compensated by direct income transfers. In this light, it would not have made sense to have established Cohesion Funds for the richer newcomers (Austria, Finland and Sweden) but it will be quite sensible to transfer those funds to the new Eastern European members.

We shall return in Chapter 5 to consider how accession of poorer countries affected social policies within the richer incumbent members of the EU. Here, we find it useful to look at how the accession affected the economic performance in the poorer countries.[64] Information on macroeconomic performance of the four cohesion countries *vis-à-vis* the EU15 average over a 20-year period is provided in Table 4.2. In terms of income, their degree of convergence is mixed. Ireland is the clear success story, having gone from an income of 61% of the EC average at the time of accession to 98% in 1996. Progress has been slower in the remaining cases, namely Greece (from 54% to 66%), Portugal (59% to 68%) and Spain (70% to 77%). Given this report's focus, in our discussion of the impact of accession we stress economic integration, via trade and FDI flows, and at the end of the sub-section turn to social policy in the new entrants. It is worth noting that the accession of Portugal and Spain took place simultaneously with the run up for the Single Market programme. Since these two events should have similar effects in many cases, e.g. increases in trade and FDI flows between these two countries with the remaining EU members, it is difficult to ascertain the the separate effects of accession.

Figures 4.1 and 4.2 display employment growth and relative unemployment for ten years either side of the accession date. Unemployment rates are measured relative to a 'core' of large long-standing EU members (the average of Germany, France and Italy) so as to control for the effect of generally rising unemployment throughout the EU (in other words we want to know whether the entrants did better or worse than existing members); business cycle effects are also filtered out of the individual country data.[65] Figure 4.1 suggests that there was little effect of EU accession on employment growth in Greece or Portugal, but a positive effect in Spain and Ireland. Figure 4.2 suggests accession was associated with a subsequent rise in (relative) unemployment rates in Spain and Greece and a decrease in Ireland and Portugal.

The variety in the impact of integration among the cohesion countries can be attributed both to the structural characteristics of each country, and to the shares in output and employment of the sectors which were more sensitive to higher competition. Despite

Table 4.2 Main economic indicators for Social Cohesion countries

	1974–85	*1986–90*	*1991–6*
GDP growth			
Greece	2.5	1.9	1.2
Ireland	3.8	4.6	4.7
Portugal	2.2	5.1	1.1
Spain	1.9	4.5	1.4
EU 15	2.0	3.3	1.4
Inflation			
Greece	17.7	16.5	13.6
Ireland	12.8	3.2	2.0
Portugal	20.8	13.3	8.8
Spain	15.0	7.4	5.1
EU 15	10.5	4.9	3.7
Real unit labour costs[1]			
Greece	1.0	–0.8	0.7
Ireland	0.2	–2.1	–2.0
Portugal	–0.4	1.1	–0.4
Spain	0.1	3.2	–2.4
EU 15	–1.9	5.4	–2.4
Employment growth			
Greece	1.0	0.9	0.9
Ireland	0.1	1.0	1.7
Portugal	–0.4	1.1	–0.4
Spain	–1.4	3.3	–0.1
EU 15	0.0	1.3	–0.5
Unemployment rate			
Greece	3.8	6.6	8.3
Ireland	10.6	15.5	14.7
Portugal	6.9	6.1	5.6
Spain	11.3	18.9	20.8
EU 15	6.4	9.0	10.3

[1] Relative unit labour costs in common currency (annual % change) against other member countries; in the case of EU15, against 9 other OECD countries.
Source: Eurostat, *Basic Statistics of the EU*, Luxembourg (various issues).

sharing a number of characteristics, such as a large share of agriculture (15–25% of total employment, compared to 8% in the EU as a whole), an underdeveloped physical infrastructure, and a sizeable

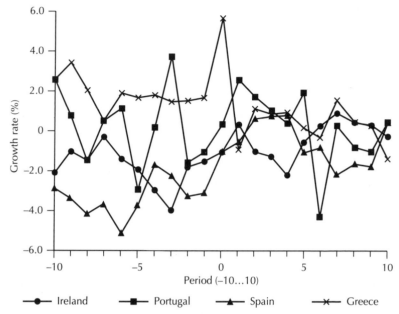

Figure 4.1 Employment growth rates (relative to EU core)
* Both employment growth rates have been HP filtered.

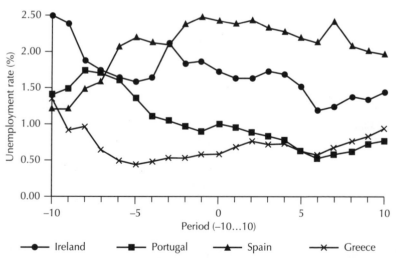

Figure 4.2 Unemployment rates (relative to EU core)
* Both unemployment rates have been HP filtered.

small firm sector, etc., the relative importance of manufacturing and services varied somewhat, and it was therefore to be expected that their economies would react differently to integration. With the opening up of both domestic and foreign markets, the successful industries expanded through capturing increased market share in the EU market, while unsuccessful ones contracted due to loss of market share in the domestic market. Moreover, the initial degree of openness of each of these economies was different, with Ireland being already very open, and Greece and Spain being rather closed (see Table 4.3).

Table 4.3 Basic economic facts on Social Cohesion countries at accession

Country (accession date)	GDP per capita[1]	Openness[2]	Farming population	Foreign direct investment[3]
Ireland (1973)	60.8	76.6	24.1	5.3
Greece (1981)	54.2	38.9	30.8	1.0
Portugal (1986)	58.5	61.2	23.8	1.9
Spain (1986)	69.6	37.1	16.2	1.9

[1] As a percentage of EU average at the date of accession.
[2] Exports plus imports divided by GDP.
[3] Average ratio of gross foreign direct investment flows to GDP over the period 1986–96.
Sources: International Labour Organisation(1994), *Year Book of Labour Statistics*, Geneva. Eurostat (1996), *European Union Direct Investment Yearbook*, Luxembourg.

4.2.1 Structural changes and accession

The degree of openness and the structure of production of these countries was not only initially different, but also experienced important changes after accession. *Ireland* has seen the composition of its trade flows change most significantly in recent decades. For example, while food accounted for 50% of exports in 1970 this figure had dropped to 20% by 1996. At the same time, the exports in 1970 of manufactured goods increased from 25% to 70%. About three-quarters of these exports are accounted for by foreign firms which, on average, export 90% of their production in comparison with 33% for indigenous Irish firms. The foreign firms export primarily high technology products, for example, accounting for about 40% of European

PC software production. The geographical destination of exports has also varied significantly since accession to the EU. Before integration the vast majority of Irish trade was with the UK which by 1960 took 75% of Irish exports. Nowadays, this proportion has dropped to 25% whilst over the same period the share of exports going to other EU countries increased from 7% to 40%. The main influence on the diversification of trade has been the role of foreign multinational firms with marketing strategies designed to capture markets in Europe and further afield. Indeed, FDI is a crucial ingredient in Ireland's success, whose source is discussed in more detail in Box 4.1.

Box 4.1 **Irish growth and FDI**

Ireland changed from a largely inward-looking protectionist approach to a set of export-oriented and industrial policies in the late 1950s.[66] This presented enormous attraction to multinational companies (MNCs), with membership of the EU in 1973 further confirming Ireland's attractiveness as an industrial location. The Export Profits Tax Relief Scheme introduced in the 1950s, under which manufacturers exporting their products were freed from taxation on the profits from export sales, was abolished in 1981 for anti-competitive reasons. The 1969 Industrial Development Act gave rise to an industrial promotion agency which could give grants towards the purchase of fixed assets up to 60% of the cost in designated areas.

By the 1980s, however, there were serious concerns that the industrial policies were not having sufficient impact in reducing unemployment, calling for a greater control over the process of industrial development. The legislation shifted the emphasis somewhat from funding fixed assets towards developing export markets, the acquisition of technology and R&D. After a period of severe fiscal and debt difficulties during the late 1970s and 1980s, there was a strong process of fiscal consolidation, with the Public Sector borrowing requirement falling from 20% of GDP in 1981 to 3% of GDP in 1989.

All these policies have led to rapid growth driven primarily by a very dynamic export sector dominated by MNCs which serve as a conduit for the adoption of advanced technologies. For example, foreign firms now account for almost 50% of total manufacturing jobs, compared to 30% twenty years ago. The boom in FDI flows reflects many things ranging from Ireland's attractiveness as a natural base for exports to the EU and the availability of a highly skilled and English-speaking labour force, to the provision of generous tax incentives. Two factors in particular explain the success in attracting FDI in recent years: the renewed interest of American and European firms in gaining a foothold in Europe to take advantage of the extension of the EU in 1986 (and later in 1995) and the completion of the Single Market in 1992; and the clear move to macroeconomic stability that took place in the late 1980s. An additional consideration is the inflow of large subsidies from the EU (peaking in 1979 at 6% of GDP and then gradually falling to about 4%) which has helped to finance infrastructure and educational investment without causing budgetary problems. For example, by 1996, Irish receipts from the EU amounted to 4.2% of Irish GDP, out of which 63% was due to CAP and 22% to Structural and Cohesion Funds.

Portugal has also witnessed a drastic change in the geographical pattern of its trade flows during the last decade. The proportion of intra-EU trade has risen from 48% to 75%. In this respect, it is important to emphasize the role of textiles which contributes 30% of export earnings. The combination of low labour costs, EU investment incentives and a favourable local tax regime has provided an attractive environment for foreign investment, with FDI flows in recent years averaging 3–4% of GDP. The annual inflow of FDI more than doubled as a share of total investment compared to the 1980–5 period. In contrast to Ireland, however, the largest increases in FDI flows occurred in the non-tradable sector (construction, banking and insurance, and services) as most foreign firms sought to take advantage of opportunities in the domestic market. On the other hand, there has been selective FDI in some sectors with a strong export orientation (food and beverages, electrical engineering) which have affected the specialization within Portuguese manufacturing.

Being the largest of the periphery economies, *Spain* had a highly diversified industrial structure and the importance of sectors sensitive to integration was lower than in Portugal and Greece. Intra-industry trade intensified, particularly in products of medium and low quality and in sectors with strong or intermediate demand at the EU level. Western Europe has always been the most important market for Spanish trade, a fact which was reinforced after EC accession. Exports to the EU have increased their share from 52% in 1986 to 67% in 1991. On the exports side, foodstuffs gradually lost their share, while durable consumer goods (especially cars) exported to the EU and capital goods to Latin-American countries, increased their importance. With regard to imports, capital goods have increased their share in total imports from 11% in 1985 to 24% in 1996. FDI flows increased strongly after accession, growing from 1.2% of GDP in 1986 to 4.2% in 1991, and falling thereafter, being mostly concentrated in manufacturing (43%) and the financial sector (35%).

During the 1970s the pattern of exports in *Greece* shifted from minerals and agricultural products to manufactured products (textiles and metals) which nowadays account for 55% of all exports, while machinery and transport equipment accounts for 65% of imports. This trend reflected the emphasis on industrial development but also a barter trade agreement with the Eastern bloc states and the use of a 1% levy on bank loans to subsidize exports. These trade-assisting devices disappeared upon accession, contributing to a sharp decline in manufacturing performance in the 1980s. In contrast to Portugal and Spain, inward flows of FDI increased only slightly and were concentrated in just one region (Attica).

4.2.2 Employment and the role of changing policies in the cohesion countries

Let us now turn to labour market performance. As illustrated in Figures 4.1 and 4.2, the consequences of accession on this score have been far from uniformly positive in the four countries. In the case of *Spain*, unemployment is currently hovering below 20%, and has never fallen below 16% since the mid-1980s. Much of the blame lies with a panoply of rules that have made Spain's labour market one of the most rigid in the world. For example, firing employees is very costly and the route taken to alleviate this problem was to create a two-tier labour market: well-protected insiders with permanent contracts and outsiders on temporary contracts with low firing costs. Because the insiders were insulated from the risk of job loss, high unemployment did little to moderate wage demands.[67] Relatively long unemployment benefits and a compressed wage structure aggravated by sectoral/regional collective bargaining also served to keep joblessness high.

According to Chapter 1, the areas where the EU social policy impinges on the legal authority of member states are rather marginal for the overall functioning of the labour market. In this sense, it is difficult to find concrete instances in which EU regulations forced Spain to adopt social standards that were significantly higher than the ones they had anyway. The only changes that took place were in relation to the directive on the obligations of employers about informing workers on their labour contract conditions, the directive on European works councils and the directive on parental leave. While these instances are not significant enough to have much influence on overall labour market performance, major pre-enlargement changes in Spanish labour market legislation did have their origin in the expected consequences of accession. For instance, the 1984 extension of the scope for using fixed-term contracts, although implemented at the trough of a recession, was also clearly influenced by the perspective of joining the EC in the mid-1980s. This reform appears to have helped employment growth after accession, in the boom of the second half of the 1980s, but also to have fostered job destruction in the subsequent recession. The resulting two-tier labour market has also had adverse side-effects like a higher wage pressure and a fall in productivity, leading to further reforms in 1994 and 1997 aimed at curtailing the degree of segmentation. Likewise, the significant increase in the generosity of unemployment benefits in 1984 can be interpreted as an effort to catch up with the prevailing systems in more advanced EU countries. It has had a negative effect on the persistence of high unemployment in Spain, where long-term unemployment is about 50% of total unemployment,[68] and jeopardized the sustainability of the social security system. The latter led to reforms, starting in 1992, restricting access to unemployment benefits and increasing social security contributions on employers.

Greece shares some of the characteristics of the Spanish labour market. High wage demands following the end of dictatorship jacked up real wages twice as fast as any improvement in productivity. A fully-fledged welfare system, comprising generous unemployment benefits, a minimum wage, and high severance payments were introduced prior to accession and then strengthened by the socialist government elected in 1981. At the very moment when other EC

States were turning away from policies such as nationalization, the maintenance of employment through support to declining industries and fiscal expansion, Greece embraced them. The intensified external competition associated with EC membership combined to produce low growth and major macroeconomic imbalances by the late 1980s. The swing back to a liberal-conservative government 1991–3 and the subsequent adjustment programme supported by an EC loan of 2.2 billion ECU, introduced a wide-ranging package of liberalizing reforms (mainly privatization) which ended abruptly in 1993 with the return of the socialist party to power, although the current socialist administration is committed to liberalization policies. The effects of all these changes on the labour market appear to have been minor with unemployment rising from 6% in the 1980s to just 8% in the 1990s; however, these figures are somewhat misleading in disguising wide underemployment in agriculture and the informal urban sector.

Ireland has had better labour market performance than Spain or Greece. This reflects not only macroeconomic factors, but also policy features. At a general level, Irish policies were not particularly liberal, indeed they were almost exactly the opposite of those implemented in the UK during the early 1980s: high personal taxes, generous welfare provisions, a top-down industrial strategy and a strong incomes policy in the form of social contracts. These contracts, signed by the government, unions and employers, deserve much of the credit for the durability of the recovery since the mid-1980s, however. Without wage restraint, the country's high growth rate would surely have raised inflation, something which has not so far occurred. To complete the virtuous circle, however, higher productivity was also needed, which came in the form of industrial policy. In this respect, the story of Ireland's success is a tale of two economies: a backward, labour-intensive one owned by the Irish, and a modern, capital-intensive one largely owned by foreigners. The rise in productivity has also increased labour force participation and reversed the direction of migration from outwards to inwards. Partly as a result of this increase in the labour supply, unemployment remains substantial, despite the robust employment growth.

Portugal also provides a very useful example for comparison with Spain. In contrast with its neighbour's case, real wage flexibility is high in Portugal. This combines with a high level of employment rigidity which, as in the Spanish case, stems from the way industrial relations took place under dictatorship. Consequently, labour market adjustment usually starts through wage movement, while employment is subject to significant lags. Labour costs are low, about one-half of Spain's. Coverage of unemployment benefits was widened at the beginning of the 1990s in an attempt to improve the welfare state, but it still remains ten percentage points lower than in Spain. Furthermore, minimum wage legislation was introduced in the mid-1970s and currently affects only about 3% of the work-force. Since the mid-1980s, the government has developed a non-statutory prices and incomes policy, wrapped up with improvements in the minimum wage and tax relief. The lack of any agreements in 1994–5 led to real wage stagnation, which helped the disinflationary process that took place. Current unemployment is about 7%; however, this figure does not take account of the high levels of underemployment in agriculture and in parts of the public sector. If short-time working were included, Portugal's unemployment would be much closer to the EU average.

The unemployment experiences of Portugal and Spain are particularly interesting to compare.[69] In Spain the reduction of inflation from 10% to the current 2% took 15 years and was associated with a rise of 13 percentage points in unemployment, whereas in Portugal it was accomplished in only five years and with hardly any extra unemployment. Despite the outward similarities in labour market institutions, there are several differences which could explain such stark contrast. First, before 1985 Spain enjoyed a generous system of unemployment benefits, while Portugal had none; after 1989, the benefit systems look more similar, although Spain still has a higher coverage rate and longer benefit durations. Second, minimum wages (set by collective bargaining) are higher, *vis-à-vis* average wages, in Spain. Finally, firing costs are also higher in Spain. Combined, these three factors create greater real wage rigidity in Spain than in Portugal and provide a good illustration of the problems that a lack of flexibility in labour markets may cause the former Communist Central and Eastern Europe Countries (CEECs) if they are required to adopt stringent labour market regulations as the price of joining the European club.

4.2.3 Lessons

The preceding discussion suggests two broad conclusions. As regards trade patterns, the lesson is that there have been shifts in specialization from unskilled labour-intensive products to higher value-added ones. The industrialization programmes which have taken place since accession have, however, somehow failed to attract labour-intensive industries and to integrate the successful foreign-based sectors with the domestic sectors which were concentrated in specific regions (like Andalucia, the second poorest region in Spain). In this respect, there is evidence[70] showing that around half of the income inequality present across (NUTS2) EU regions corresponds to differences between regions within each country. Also, although income differentials across EU countries have narrowed during the 1980s, differentials across regions within each member state have widened. In this sense, had it not been for the Social Cohesion Funds, the inequalities would have been even larger.

As to labour market performance, the main lesson from the enlargement experience is that a rigid labour market like that of Spain appears ill suited to dealing with the structural changes that inevitably accompany accession and, more generally, that a comprehensive European-style safety net may not be well suited to the special needs of poor countries joining a free trade area. In particular, this experience suggests that some aspects of the *acquis* are best phased in slowly, after the bulk of the transition has been implemented and when living standards have converged significantly towards those obtaining in the rest of the EU. While EU membership must ultimately involve the same status for entrants as for existing members, there is no reason why different aspects of membership should not be phased in at different speeds.

4.3 Enlargement to the East

We now turn to the question of future enlargement, in particular to incorporate the CEECs. Association accords were signed with Poland, Hungary and Czechoslovakia in December 1991; in 1993 Romania and Bulgaria (and the newly formed Czech and Slovak Republics) also became associated countries, with an aim to create a freed trade area. Accession of a 'fast track' group of five CEECs[71] (the Czech Republic, Estonia, Hungary, Poland and Slovenia) is unlikely before 2005. The remaining applicants – Bulgaria, Latvia, Lithuania, Romania and Slovakia – will have to wait even longer.

Table 4.4 contains some basic economic facts for both sets of countries, together with the richest and poorest current member

Table 4.4 Basic economic facts in Central and Eastern European countries and selected EU countries (1996)

	GDP per capita[1] (% of EU average)	Population (thousands)	Unemploy-ment rate (%)	Partici-pation rate (%, 16–65)	GDP growth (%)	Farming population (%)	Hourly labour cost[2] (US $)
CEECs							
Fast track							
Czech Rep.	57.0	10.5	3.6	77.2	4.4	11.0	4.7
Estonia	22.0	1.5	9.6	66.2	4.0	14.0	3.6
Hungary	37.0	10.5	10.8	61.2	0.8	8.0	2.6
Poland	31.0	39.0	12.7	66.7	6.0	26.9	1.9
Slovenia	59.0	2.0	9.7	70.3	3.1	6.0	2.4
Slow track							
Bulgaria	24.4	8.4	18.1	72.6	–5.2	23.2	2.1
Latvia	18.3	2.5	9.5	74.0	0.9	18.5	1.6
Lithuania	24.0	3.7	8.7	76.2	2.1	23.8	2.2
Romania	25.2	22.7	8.2	78.3	1.1	34.4	2.0
Slovak Rep.	41.2	5.4	12.7	74.2	2.3	9.7	4.2
EU	**100.0**	**372.0**	**10.9**	**67.5**	**1.8**	**5.3**	**15.0**
Denmark	116.0	5.2	7.8	78.5	2.5	4.4	19.6
Germany	110.0	81.0	9.2	71.1	1.6	3.2	23.0
France	106.8	58.0	12.3	67.1	1.5	4.9	17.3
Italy	104.6	57.2	12.0	60.1	0.7	7.5	15.2
UK	97.0	58.0	8.2	75.8	2.1	1.1	13.2
Ireland	97.7	3.6	15.0	61.6	6.2	12.6	12.9
Spain	77.0	39.2	21.9	59.2	2.2	9.3	12.8
Portugal	68.3	10.0	7.2	68.5	3.0	11.5	6.1
Greece	65.9	10.4	9.8	58.6	2.6	20.4	5.8

[1] European purchasing power parity, 1996.
[2] 1994.

Sources: OECD, *National Accounts* (various issues), International Labour Organisation, *Year Book of Labour Statistics* (various issues).

states of the EU. The fast track group has an average GDP per head which is only a third of the average for current member states. By contrast, GDP per head in Greece, the poorest current member of the EU, is still two-thirds that of the EU average. The CEECs in the second group, with the exception of Slovakia, are even poorer with an average GDP per head of only one-fifth of the EU average. There are 63.5 million people in the fast track group – nearly 17% of the current EU population – while the second group represents an extra 43 million people. Both sets of countries are also far more agricultural, with farming populations about twice the EU average in the first group and about four times in the second one.

4.3.1 CEEC experiences and prospects

Issues arising within the CEECs have been admirably discussed in a recent CEPR Report,[72] and we can do no better than simply recall some of the main points made there. Enlargement to the East raises many of the same issues, albeit on a larger scale, to those confronted in the 1980s when the Mediterranean countries joined the EU. The prospects are potentially good for both the existing members of the EU and the new entrants. For the CEECs, linking their fortunes to the EU offers the prospect of enjoying the high and rising living standards of the West. For the EU, continuing economic success in the East can help foster prosperity throughout the continent. There is, however, also an unfavourable side in the return of CEECs to Europe. Restructuring in the East has initially been associated with rising unemployment and stagnant or falling incomes, which could foster widespread disillusion with a market system and provoke mass migration. Additionally, the process of integration with the West will lead to restructuring there, and the likelihood of charges of social dumping and countervailing protectionist policies.

For all its inefficiencies, central planning had some virtues: job security was high, essential benefits were guaranteed, pay structures were remarkably egalitarian, labour force participation was high and unemployment was apparently very low. Alongside these strengths there were major weaknesses (in many cases a direct consequence of these same policies): wages bore no relation to productivity which itself was low, the low levels of open unemployment were only achieved through high levels of hidden unemployment, the system of wage bargaining contributed to inflationary pressures, employment was excessively concentrated in industry and agriculture, and labour mobility was very limited.

As a consequence of the transition process, those weaknesses became much more apparent. Full employment was no longer sustainable, and output collapsed, for both supply and demand-related reasons. State-owned firms began shedding unwanted labour, first by attrition and later in the course of privatization by mass layoffs. With price liberalization, many of the goods previously produced were no longer in demand. Trade arrangements among centrally planned economies collapsed in 1991, leading many State firms to lose their Eastern Europe export markets. On the other hand, newly created private firms could not grow fast enough, lacking capital and expertise, and therefore could not offset the fall in the demand for labour. Real wages adjusted downwards, but even at low levels unemployment increased in most countries to a two-digit figure. Labour supply also declined strongly, as an increasing number of workers withdrew from the labour force. As a result of these developments, systemic dependency ratios have risen sharply, bloating social security budgets and raising the tax burden on those in conventional paid employment. This in turn has raised the relative attractiveness of working in the underground economy, aggravating the problem further.

Accession to the EU contains risks as well as rewards.[73] The applicants lack the industrial base and expenditure levels of richer EU member states. Yet in many cases their geographical proximity to central EU markets, along with their comparatively low costs and skilled labour force, help to compensate for their disadvantages, and have allowed them to attract large inward investment flows. Over the next few years more firms can be expected to settle in the CEECs, in turn creating positive externalities that will attract further investments. A recent study[74] estimates the gains to be large for the applicants (23–50 billion ECU at 1992 prices, including farm and Structural Fund transfers), and small and unevenly distributed for the current EU member states (Germany being the biggest gainer).

Two risks could prevent these gains being realized. First, real wages are presently much lower in the CEECs than in the current EU, and indeed given productivity levels this needs to be so if inward FDI is to take place on a significant scale. If full labour mobility within an enlarged EU were introduced straight away, however, then significant labour migration to the West might occur. We suggested in Chapter 2 that skilled workers might be more likely to move than unskilled ones, but an outflow of skilled labour is probably the last thing the CEECs need at this juncture. In fact, there has been some movement away from the artificially low wage dispersion which was typical of centrally planned economies. For instance, in Poland a worker at the bottom of the top decile in the wage distribution received 97% more than the median worker in 1995, as compared to 59% in 1989, while a worker at the top of the bottom decile got 59% of the median wage, as compared to 66% in 1989. These relativities are similar to those in the UK. Similarly, in Slovenia the highest wage admitted in collective agreements was 13 times the minimum wage in 1996, whereas it was only 5 times in 1989. The current OECD ratio is of the order of 20 to 1.[75] Notice, however, that measures of inequality based upon wages/earnings obviously exclude the unemployed, and hence may be downward biased, particularly if unemployment has risen a lot, as is the case in many CEECs. Moreover, the returns to possessing skills in these countries are still significantly lower than in EU countries. Thus, there is something to be said for introducing full labour mobility only within the enlarged EU later – in other words encouraging physical capital to flow in rather than human capital to flow out.

In practice, however, even if labour mobility were introduced early on, migratory flows might be limited by countervailing policy responses in the West of the EU. As noted in Chapter 2, even though it might be the skilled who leave the East, in the West they would be competing with relatively unskilled workers, depressing their wages or driving them into unemployment. At that point policies to protect the 'nearest poor' would swing into action, as in the posted workers example of Box 3.3. Even so, it seems better to manage the transition by a gradual removal of barriers to labour mobility, rather than an immediate removal of formal barriers coupled with the imposition of informal ones.

The second risk lies at the other extreme, namely wage equalization, for a way to prevent migration is obviously the elevation of wages to EU levels. This is desirable as a long-run equilibrium outcome, but one should not try to impose it before productivity levels have also converged; that would simply be a recipe for low investment and rocketing unemployment. German reunification provides a clear example of how integration can homogenize wages across regions that vary greatly in their attractiveness to business, with dramatic effects on unemployment: wages in the East rose by 42% between the first quarter of 1990 and October of that same year, while unemployment increased from 2% in 1990 to 11% in 1991. Factors contributing to this wage inflation included: union pressure for wage equalization so as to prevent large scale migration; large increases in social security contributions; and a perception on the part of the workers that higher unemployment in the East did not justify lower wages.[76]

It is true that the pressure for higher wages in the new applicants will not be as strong as in the case of German reunification. Some of the forces that drove East German wages up so rapidly will still be present, however. In this respect, early harmonization of labour market practices in the entrants with those of the current member states would inevitably increase their labour costs. Some of the possible effects are illustrated by the 'new economic geography' literature. This focuses on the countervailing forces played by transport costs – a force for separation – and market size – a force for agglomeration. Integration – effectively lowering transport costs – tends to lead to greater concentration of economic activity as agglomeration effects become relatively more important. If labour costs are also equalized across regions even though their production structures are initially quite different, then the result can be an aggravation, rather than amelioration, of regional inequalities, because the less industrialized regions simply cannot compensate for their smaller local markets and scarcity of local suppliers by having lower labour costs.[77] This insight is obviously relevant to the imposition of the social *acquis* on the CEECs, which we address below.

4.3.2 A policy dilemma

Integration of the CEECs poses a particularly thorny policy dilemma for the EU. Their low labour costs and highly skilled labour forces give them the chance to become Europe's tiger economies. The dilemma is that their success may at the same time imply adverse distributional consequences for the current EU members. Their comparative advantage currently lies in labour-intensive industries, so a likely result of integration would be a sizeable increase of exports in these goods from the CEECs to present EU members; the consequence would be a fall in the employment and wages of the least skilled workers in current EU members. If their nearest poor are hurt in this fashion, EU citizens are liable to reject the enlargement process and/or raise their demands for trade protection against CEEC products, possibly through demands for higher labour standards in the CEECs to prevent 'social dumping'.

From the point of view of the CEECs, a few key ingredients for success can be pointed out. First, a successful transition will inevitably be accompanied by major restructuring away from inefficient manufacturing industries and State-owned enterprises; natural counterparts to this process should be appropriate training programmes and unemployment benefit regimes to support the workers made redundant (although the structure needs to be such as not to inhibit job search). Second, the CEECs will benefit from unfettered access to Western markets, so as to boost growth and speed the process of labour reallocation. Third, free labour mobility into the West could also help, both as a safety valve against unemployment and as a means to acquiring skills which are scarce back home. Besides opening up their markets to CEEC producers and lowering their barriers to migrants from the East, EU countries could also assist the development process in at least two other ways: the private sector, by channelling FDI to the CEECs, and the EU, by funding the aforementioned training and social programmes to ease the process.

Although current EU members gain from the integration of the CEECs by reaping the gains from trade stressed in Chapter 1, each of these ingredients could be associated with adverse distributional effects. Increased import penetration in industries such as coal, steel and shipbuilding will further depress the demand for workers with traditional or no skills. The less skilled would also be adversely affected by immigration of Eastern Europeans on a scale which, given current per capita income differences in Table 4.4, could be of the large 1960s variety, rather than the trickle of the 1980s that followed the Portuguese and Spanish accession. Some indication that this would be the case is given by the present recorded flows, which as Table 4.5 indicates are becoming sizeable, even with the current high barriers to migration. Strong FDI would prompt precisely the type of establishment relocations that is the stuff of newspaper headlines mentioned at the top of this chapter, but on an even bigger scale. Lastly, since the EU budget is presently capped at 1.27% of EU GDP, transfers to the new members imply a reduction of subsidies for current members, both those paid as guaranteed prices to farmers under the Common Agricultural Policy and those paid to the poorest EU regions under the Structural Funds, particularly in the Cohesion four.

In the face of these potential distributional effects one can expect to see four countervailing responses: overt protectionism; barriers to migration; meanness in financial support; and the imposition of social clauses on new members. First, the accession agreements are likely to impose barriers to trade and labour mobility, in the form of

Table 4.5 Net migration rates in the Central and Eastern
European countries (Annual averages 1990–6)

	Net migration rate per thousand population	*Net migration thousands*
Fast track		
Czech Republic	0.5	5.2
Estonia	–3.9	–6.1
Hungary	–2.0	–20.6
Poland	–1.3	–50.0
Slovenia	–3.1	–5.9
Slow track		
Bulgaria	–2.6	–22.0
Latvia	–6.9	–18.0
Lithuania	–2.7	–10.0
Romania	–3.5	–80.0
Slovak Republic	–1.3	–7.2

Sources: United Nations (1996), *World Population Prospects*, New York. World Bank (1997) *Atlas*, Washington, DC.

long transition periods after formal accession. The EU has the upper hand in the accession negotiations and existing member countries can easily agree to remain both protectionist and closed to Eastern migrants, at least for relatively long periods. This is the opposite of what is desirable for the CEECs, at least as far as trade is concerned, where access to EU markets is essential if FDI inflows – a major springboard for growth – are to be significant.

As to financial support, in March 1998 the European Commission put forth a proposal for the EU budget over the period 2000–2006 – the *Agenda 2000*. It proposed reform of the Common Agricultural Policy in the form of a reduction in guaranteed agricultural prices and the partial replacement of price support by subsidies to farmers' incomes; this proposal provoked noisy demonstrations by farmers and their supporters in several EU countries. It also proposed a tightening of the criteria for eligibility for support from the Structural Funds; at present some 51% of the population of the EU live in regions eligible for Objective 1–5 status and this would fall to 38%. The amount of cash available for disbursement under the Structural Funds to existing members would consequently fall by 20%, allowing

Box 4.2 **Poland on the road to the EU**

The five fast-track CEECs are a motley group. Some, like Slovenia and Estonia, are so small that the EU will barely register their presence. Then there is Poland, which is a front-runner for political reasons but will be the club's trickiest newcomer. With a population of 39 million, the EU has never taken in a country both as backward and as big as Poland. The closest precedent was Spain's accession in 1986, with an almost identical population, but whose income per head at the time was 70% of the EU and whose farming population about two-thirds of Poland's current one.[78] Furthermore when Spain and Portugal joined in 1986, the EC was not yet a Single Market for goods, services, labour and capital, and both countries were already established market economies. Poland may be a 'functioning market economy', but much of it is still hobbled by statist habits. Thousands of firms will be hurt by the advent of free trade with Western Europe. Hundreds of thousands of workers in State-owned enterprises will have to find new jobs when their industries are exposed to the full force of domestic and international competition. Millions of retirees will receive smaller pensions than they had expected, and the prospects for millions of farmers will be uncertain at best.

With or without accession to the EU, Poland will have to confront these difficulties, and the prospect of EU membership merely forces the pace. Accession, however, carries costs as well as benefits. The Polish government estimates that adoption of the worker protection rules in the EU's Social Chapter will initially cost around 2–3% of GDP a year,[79] but these costs will decline as more of the restructuring process is completed and income and wage differentials with the rest of the EU narrow. It therefore makes sense for the Poles to seek to postpone introduction of the most burdensome requirements in the Chapter. The prospects in *Agenda 2000*, by denying most direct support payments to farmers in the new entrants and establishing a ceiling of 4% of GDP on the maximum any country can receive from the Structural Funds, are not good either. In this sense, Europe's reluctance to pay more or to trade freely with countries such as Poland that have lower social and environmental standards as Poland, may give rise to threats of transition periods even longer than those for Spain and Portugal, which had to wait for seven years before their citizens could work freely elsewhere in the EU.

Nonetheless, accession carries great potential. As indicated in the text, accession and economic integration prompted an investment boom in Spain and Portugal as production shifted to exploit comparative advantage. Some of this is already happening in Poland, which is growing at 6% a year, one of the fastest rates in Europe, and foreign investment is pouring in. Yet to lift Poland's living standards from less than a third of the EU average now, these high growth rates will have to be sustained over decades. Premature imposition of inflexibilities will merely prevent this happening.

funds of around 46 billion ECU to be diverted to the CEECs (plus Cyprus). The share of the budget going to these countries would then reach 11%, or around 0.14% of EU15 GDP, by 2006. These proposals for reform of the Structural Funds have in turn triggered several rounds of negotiations between the Commission and the governments of the Cohesion countries.

What should we expect in the near future? Before commenting on future scenarios we should start by noting that in some dimensions several of the CEECs have overcome the initial phase of transition. For example, recent evidence from 'gravity' models for trade show that countries like Poland and the Czech Republic nowadays have trade/GDP ratios of comparable magnitude to EU counterparts of similar population size like Spain and Austria, and that such ratios are not likely to increase much in the near future.[80] Thus, following trade liberalization in 1991, the openness of those CEECs has already become similar to that in other EU countries, without creating insurmountable problems to the EU member states. In other words, the message for EU policy-makers is that most of the redirection of trade has already taken place and that there is no need for a long adjustment period with special protection concerning trade.

In the longer run, however, the scope for increased export growth to EU markets depends on whether a catching-up process takes place in the CEECs and this will depend upon factors which facilitate the process of industrial restructuring. In this respect, the impact will be felt through a number of channels. First, accession implies both structural adjustment and institutional change, and the ambiguous impact on employment and unemployment of the EU's southern enlargement discussed earlier suggests caution. Secondly, as the environment stabilizes low real unit labour costs may prove increasingly attractive to foreign investors, with a beneficial impact on the CEECs, but possibly undesirable consequences on the rest of the EU and particularly in those EU countries which are labour intensive. Although the evidence on the effects of trade in inequality is scarce in Europe,[81] there is abundant evidence for the US which points out that the idea that trade has caused increased inequality does not square well with the facts, and that technological-bias may be a much more important factor.[82] As regards the Social Cohesion countries, however, there is evidence, for instance regarding Spain,[83] that inequality has increased. In particular, pre-tax earnings inequality increased in the second half of the 1980s and the 1990s, even though after-tax earnings inequality decreased (though whether this is the result of foreign trade is uncertain). Given that these inequality measures apply to employed workers only, and therefore exclude the unemployed (20% of the labour force), it is likely that inequality has indeed increased. Since 70% of unemployed workers are unskilled, it is also likely that opening trade with the CEECs may have worsened the job prospects of workers in low value added manufacturing sectors. Finally, as in the case of southern EU countries, where low participation rates may mask an extended 'black economy', if closer integration of the CEECs with Europe necessitates the enforcement of EU regulations on small firms, this will have an adverse short-run impact on labour demand and lead to a rise in the size of the underground economy.

5 Social Policy in the Next Millennium

Labour ministers of the 15 debated yesterday ... the social consequences of the closing of the Belgian factory of Renault at Vilvoorde ... The commissioner for Social Affairs, Padraig Flynn, proposed elaborating a 'code of conduct' ... agreed between the social partners ... to avoid similar events. The objective of this initiative is to ensure that workers are informed and consulted by the firm before restructuring. The management at Renault, argued commissioner Flynn, had violated both national and Community legislation ... Relocations and plant closings 'of this type create great social unrest and generate worker dissatisfaction with the construction of a socially strong European Union', the commissioner declared, 'that is, they give rise to social euro-skepticism'. The Belgian minister endorsed this criticism ... His German colleague asked the Commission to investigate if, in the restructuring of Renault, Community funds had in any way been used. And the French representative, who avoided confrontation, defended the elaboration of a 'common strategy' on the European social model.

(Translated from 'La UE elabora un código de conducta que evite cierres como el de Vilvoorde' ('The EU elaborates a code of conduct to avoid closures like Vilvoorde'), *El País Digital*, April 18, 1997.)

5.1 Forces for change

In the concluding chapter of this report we look at the various forces shaping EU social policy in the early years of the next millennium, drawing on our earlier analysis. The most relevant ones will likely be greater competition in product markets, increased intra-European migration and the introduction of the Euro.

5.1.1 Increased competition

The volume of world trade in goods has grown 15-fold since 1950, while world output is but five and a half times larger. Within Europe the degree of openness within the EU12, measured as the average of intra-EU imports and exports compared to GDP, has increased from a little over a 17% in 1958 to nearly 30% today. This is evidence of the greater integration in both the world and European economies. Tighter integration is bound to put growing pressure on the current regime of heavy regulation of labour markets and high social protection as businesses seek out the most profitable location for production.

Evidence for this hypothesis is provided by what happened in the run up to the completion of the Single Market, where the late 1980s and early 1990s saw a wave of partial labour reforms in the direction of greater labour market flexibility. The reforms were not wholesale, but rather piecemeal in nature, mainly allowing for employment on more flexible terms with reduced worker rights, such as part-time and fixed-term contracts. This strategy was politically feasible because, while preserving the rights of the majority of workers who were permanent employees in full-time jobs (the 'insiders'), it also simultaneously provided firms with greater flexibility in employment and working hours at the margin.[84]

Each country followed its own route, depending on its economic and political situation. More specifically, the rise in part-time jobs has been widespread, but of varying intensity across countries, with the largest proportions reached in the Netherlands (38% of all employees in 1996), the UK and Sweden (both around 25%). Fixed-term contracts have especially been promoted in Spain (34%), Finland (17%) and France (13%). The Italians introduced increased flexibility by weakening, and eventually abolishing, their wage indexation system (the *Scala Mobile*) and by restricting access to the wage supplementation scheme for the temporarily unemployed (the *Cassa Integrazione Guadagni*). Sweden, on the other hand, only showed signs of pursuing greater flexibility in 1993, after a sharp fall in employment.[85] One common trend can, however, be discerned: since 1986 the minimum wage, as a fraction of average earnings, has fallen in all EU countries bar Luxembourg (although we do not have data for Ireland and Finland).[86]

Increased integration also took its toll on social protection, albeit to a smaller extent. From 1980 to 1993, social expenditure as a share of GDP in the EU12 rose on average by 3.3 percentage points, with falls in only Belgium, the former West Germany and Luxembourg. The rate of increase slowed *vis-à-vis* the 1970s, however. Indeed between 1983 and 1989 the EU12 governments, aided by robust growth, managed to reduce the share of social protection in GDP from 26.2% to 24.9%, but the early 1990s recession pushed it back to an all-time high of 27.6% in 1994. More recently, in meeting the deficit criteria of the Maastricht Treaty, governments have again tried to contain costs. Measures include the tightening of eligibility conditions, reducing benefit rates and increased targeting. For example, in respect of unemployment benefits, while there was little change in the level and duration of unemployment benefits in the first half of the 1990s, overall generosity was reduced by tightening both work availability and eligibility requirements.[87]

Pressures on social protection policies arising from increased integration will add to strong demographic pressures. It is expected that by 2005 the population aged 65 or over will represent as much as 26% of the population of working age (15–64 years old), as compared with 23% in 1995. If the average pension remained unchanged in relation to GDP per head, this would result in an increase in expenditure from 12% to 13.5% of GDP.[88]

As to the financing of social protection, from 1980 to 1993 the burden was gradually shifted from social security contributions onto general taxation (by about 2.5 percentage points of GDP). Within the latter, the share paid by employers fell by 6 percentage points on average, a drop paid for, roughly equally, by the protected persons themselves and taxpayers in general.[89] This transfer of the tax burden away from the internationally mobile factors of production towards those less mobile is part of an unmistakable trend. For example, from 1986 to 1994 corporate tax rates have fallen in all G-7 economies bar Italy, where it remained constant.[90] On the other hand, from 1991 to 1994 the total tax wedge between labour costs and take home pay, arising from income taxes and employer and employee social security contributions, has risen in 11 out of the 15 members of the EU (i.e. excluding Austria, Denmark, Ireland and the Netherlands).[91]

It might be thought that these effects from increased competition are not very significant given that taxes and social expenditure have been on a rising trend for 50 years. As noted in Chapter 3, however, it is not straightforward to separate out demand and supply influences, and thus disentangle the interactions between tax policy, income levels, and economic behaviour. Higher income levels are associated with higher taxes (and larger investment flows), but government budgets are also larger in more internationally open countries. As noted earlier, the latter correlation is best interpreted as a reflection of a higher demand for protection by workers exposed to international competition. As the limits to redistribution are reached, further increases in the supply of protection are likely to be hampered by tax competition. Furthermore, our analysis of US tax and benefit systems indeed suggested that jurisdictional competition is associated with lower local spending.

5.1.2 **Migration**

Another important source of pressure on social policy will be labour mobility. Despite perceptions to the contrary, migration has historically been quite high within Europe. The last big wave of migration was in the 1950s and 1960s, during which 10.5 million people migrated, mostly from Southern to Northern Europe. This flow ceased after the oil price shock of 1973, when the Northern European countries, worried about rising unemployment, introduced more restrictive immigration policies. The migratory flow, however, has not resumed as a result of either the lower barriers to mobility caused by the creation of the Single Market and the enlargement of the EU, or the economic boom of the second half of the 1980s. In 1994 migrants represented 5% of the population of the EU, one-third of which were nationals from other EU member countries, and annual migration *between* EU countries was less than 0.2% of the population.[92] Data from 1991 show that the proportion of the EU labour force made up of other EU nationals ranged from less than 0.2% in Greece, Spain and Portugal to just under 3% in France and Germany; the two countries with significantly higher fractions were the countries serving as hosts to major EU institutions, namely Belgium (5.3%) and Luxembourg (31%). Interregional migration *within* EU countries is somewhat larger, at 1–1.5% of the working-age population in 1994,[93] but it is still low by US standards, where the comparable rate of interstate migration is 3%. Moreover, the interregional migration rate has also fallen within many countries: for example from 1.8% of the population in 1970 to 1.1% over 1984–8 in Germany; from 1.8% over 1968–75 to 1.6% over 1983–90 in France; and from 2% in 1981 to 1.7% in 1991 in Italy. In both the UK and Spain, however, the rate has recovered somewhat after falling until the mid-1980s.[94] Lastly, foreign migration to the EU has averaged around 0.3% of the population during the 1990s.

Given these numbers, it is tempting to dismiss any effect of migration offhand. Several factors may reverse the current trend, however. First, at the margin even potential mobility can make a big difference to economic behaviour. Thus, the mere perception that the status quo could lead to higher migration may prompt governments to take pre-emptive action, as indicated by the measures taken by the German government to avoid massive migration from the old DDR to the West. Second, unrecorded mobility may be high and rising. In particular, the International Labour Organisation calculates that 2.6 million people were living illegally in Western Europe in 1991; since then it may have doubled.[95] And the recent Schengen agreements abolishing border controls can only help raise these flows, since illegal immigrants need only search for the country where entry is easiest. Third, given the currently large disparities in income levels, and welfare in general, between the core of the EU and the aspiring applicants of Eastern Europe, sizeable increases in legal migration from the latter are likely to occur; this is an issue we discussed in Chapter 4.

As we have just seen, migration between EU countries is presently quite low. In principle it might be either higher or lower than interregional migration within countries, since the large income disparities across countries would tend to make it higher, but intercountry barriers in the form of different languages, customs and regulations would tend to make it lower. The fact that it is actually much lower suggests that the latter barriers are important. Disparity of regulations across countries may discourage people from moving, both because of the uncertainty caused by lack of information and because of the different treatment workers get from different national systems. By effectively discriminating against foreigners, regulation may therefore help prevent the type of fiscal externalities stemming from labour mobility that were touched on in Chapter 3, and thus avoid a race-to-the-bottom. The downside is that, by mitigating the competitive pressures brought about by migration, it also creates a reduction in efficiency and lessens the pressure for desirable reforms. Measures that further reduce the scope for discrimination regarding, e.g. social security systems, might therefore foster migration, which itself would reinforce the likelihood of a race-to-the-bottom. For example, regarding the possibility of 'pension shopping', the population aged 65 or over represents about 15% of the total population of the EU, although currently only 0.1% of the latter is represented by people of this age living in another EU country.

5.1.3 **Economic and Monetary Union**

EMU does not have a direct bearing on trade or social policy, but it will provide a renewed push for increased integration, with associated effects on output and jobs, and eventually on regulations and social expenditures.

EMU implies that, by foregoing its own currency, each country loses the ability to conduct an independent monetary policy and thus to change the exchange rate. This tool will be useful in the event of an economic shock that affects it differently from the other members of the currency union. Thus, the discussion of whether the benefits of a single currency (reduced transaction costs, greater price transparency, reduced exchange rate volatility, etc.) outweigh the costs has revolved around whether countries are similar enough to constitute an 'optimum currency area'. In principle, asymmetric shocks will be unlikely and/or small if, among other things, countries are highly integrated in terms of trade in goods and services, and have similar production structures and strongly correlated business cycles. Moreover, the impact of any adverse asymmetric shock on the affected region will be less significant if nominal wage and price flexibility is high or else labour mobility is high so that the unemployed workers can move to presently booming areas. In addition, compensatory interregional fiscal transfers may help to sustain demand, although much the same effect could also be achieved by appropriate national fiscal actions. The EU clearly scores rather poorly under the latter two criteria; a relevant question is therefore the likely prevalence of asymmetric shocks.[96]

Due to barriers to intra-EU trade in the past, economic activity is less regionally specialized in Europe than a fully integrated economy like the US. For instance, two-thirds of US automobile production is located in the Midwest and one-quarter in the South, whereas among the largest four EU economies, the corresponding shares range from 39% in Germany to 13% in the UK. With the Single Market and the Euro, production in Europe may well become more, rather than less, regionally specialized, and this will tend to make differential movements in business conditions more likely and independent monetary policy more rather than less useful.[97] Against this, however, the reduction in exchange rate risk and transaction costs brought by the advent of the Euro should spur intra-European trade, thus strengthening demand linkages between economies and tending to make business cycles more, rather than less, synchronized.[98]

Assuming that EMU is sustainable and increases integration, how will it affect labour market regulations and social protection? We can distinguish two types of effects.[99] On the one hand, frictions and imperfections, such as distortionary labour taxes, result in the equilibrium or natural rate of unemployment being higher than the socially optimal rate.[100] If there is nominal wage rigidity, the monetary authorities then have an incentive to inflate so as to lower unemployment, even though wage setters might correctly anticipate such actions. Undertaking reforms that bring the natural rate closer to the socially optimal rate is one way to reduce this inflation bias. By keeping inflation down, EMU will thus *reduce* the incentive to undertake such reforms.[101]

On the other hand, frictions such as labour market regulations make employment stability desirable. In this way they provide an incentive for the monetary authorities to use monetary and exchange rate policies in a beggar-thy-neighbour fashion: when a country is hit by an adverse shock, there is a temptation to let inflation rise, thus lowering real wages and exporting unemployment to one's trading partners. By preventing the use of monetary policy to offset country-specific shocks in this way, EMU *raises* the incentives for labour market reform. In simple terms, once a country has lost the 'easy option' of devaluation, it has no alternative but to tackle unemployment through supply-side measures.

Given the low inflation rates already achieved in most EU countries by the early 1990s, it seems reasonable to assume that the second effect will be more important, so that EMU will create pressure for reform. This view is reinforced by the likelihood that EMU will also affect labour market institutions such as collective bargaining. Typically, the best unemployment performance in the OECD has been found in countries with either very decentralized wage bargaining structures, like the US or Canada, or very centralized ones, like the Scandinavian countries.[102] Tighter economic integration and a loss of national economic policy independence (as implied by Economic and Monetary Union) imply, however, that centralized wage bargaining at the national level arguably becomes equivalent in the wider European context to decentralized wage bargains between employers and powerful unions.[103] Indeed, recent evidence appears to indicate, that centralization of wage bargaining has become less beneficial to individual countries' employment performance. In addition, centralized or 'corporatist' labour markets are characterized by much stronger wage compression. As we argue elsewhere in this report, widely different productivity levels make it impossible to imagine that centralized wage bargains could have the same beneficial effects at the EU level as they arguably did within the more homogeneous labour markets of the Scandinavian countries. Hence, economic integration should spur labour market reforms in the direction of more decentralized systems of wage determination. Indeed, according to the European Commission, the increased intra-EU competition following the completion of the Single Market programme has induced greater decentralization in collective bargaining across the EU, with greater scope for local negotiations and a greater degree of subsidiarity at company level, and has made both businesses and employees more aware of the need to link pay more closely to company level productivity.[104]

Given the disappointing performance of Europe's labour market institutions in sustaining high unemployment – averaging around 10% in the EU15 countries in the 1990s – the extra incentives for reform brought by EMU are good news. Nevertheless, it should be noted that some features of EMU will make reform harder, rather than easier. Supply-side reforms usually create losers, and will thus be easier to push through the fewer they are, and the faster the benefits of reform come through. Major reform is, therefore, likely to be easier in an environment of strong economic growth where the rate of job creation is correspondingly high. Isolated reforms by individual countries are really just a particular type of asymmetric shock. With national monetary policy unavailable and fiscal policy also possibly constrained under the Stability Pact, EU governments will find it difficult, if not impossible, to ensure that aggregate demand growth is sufficiently high to ensure that unemployment falls rapidly in the wake of reform. This in turn will make it much harder for the reforms to stick.

A final point is that it is not only asymmetric shocks that create a useful role for independent monetary policies, but also differential responses to shocks that are common across countries. Thus, suppose that France and the UK are hit by an adverse demand shock (such as a fall in the world demand for manufactures) that initially has very similar effects in the two countries; if nominal wages and prices are slow to adjust then expansionary macroeconomic policies will be called for in both countries. If, however, wages and prices respond more quickly in the UK with its now relatively flexible labour market, then a looser monetary or fiscal stance would be appropriate for only a short time in the UK, but for a longer time in France. Thus, it is desirable, other things equal, that the European economies respond to common shocks at a similar speed, and this provides another argument for some coordination/harmonization in labour market policies and structures.

5.2 Looking ahead

Given both the status quo and the forces for change, we conclude this chapter by discussing the most likely outcome for social policy and make some recommendations in light of the arguments presented above.

5.2.1 Political equilibria and intra-European integration

Although, as noted in Chapter 1, the current social *acquis* is far from binding in comparison with national laws, in the future the situation may well be different. A likely scenario is that the social *acquis*, henceforth referred to loosely as the Social Chapter, becomes progressively more stringent at the same time as national laws become less so. At some point in the future the Social Chapter may then become a binding floor preventing a race-to-the-bottom.

Starting with individual countries, the competitive concerns raised by EMU and the Single Market both make reform more desirable and hopefully also more politically feasible. The most likely result is a combination of more labour market flexibility, less social protection and lower taxation. Convergence along these lines need not imply harmonization, however. The welfare systems of continental European countries tend to be employment-related. Besides offering generous pensions to former workers, they seek to protect those individuals (prime-age males) who typically are already employed (and from the point of view of European law-makers should remain so). By contrast, the Anglo-Saxon and Scandinavian welfare models offer benefits on the basis of need.

Within Europe a further distinction can also be drawn: some countries protect workers from dismissal, others offer relatively generous unemployment compensation to job losers. The two policies are to a degree substitutes from the point of view of the worker: protection from job loss is all the more desirable when only scant unemployment insurance is available; and unemployment insurance is very much appreciated when weak job security provisions make joblessness a likely outcome.[105] Evidence suggests that across the EU countries, job security is inversely correlated to the coverage and level of unemployment insurance, though both are lower in the UK and other Anglo-Saxon OECD countries, and lowest of all in the US. This may be taken to indicate that most EU countries (with the notable exception of the UK) seek to offer similar levels of overall income security to their workers, but with different combinations of the two policy instruments. From the point of view of productive efficiency, the two policies have similar effects. Job security makes it difficult to destroy unprofitable jobs and unattractive to create new jobs; unemployment insurance, by increasing the reservation wage, makes it harder to attract workers to job vacancies. The evidence also suggests, however, that countries with relatively high job security and low unemployment insurance have done less well in creating jobs – whether because of a higher protection level and lower efficiency, or because of an intrinsic disadvantage of quantity-based employment security versus unemployment insurance and retraining schemes. As economic integration progresses in Europe, it is likely that countries like Italy, Spain and Portugal (with high job security and low unemployment benefits) will come under the greatest competitive pressure to change.

Regarding taxation and social spending, we discussed in Chapter 3 some lessons from the US. First, where there was potential competition between States (on sales taxes) differences in tax rates were indeed low, although some did remain reflecting compensating differentials; income taxes are of course mainly determined at the Federal level. Second, the key feature that prevented the race-to-the-bottom in social provision was the fact that most such spending was on Federal rather than State programmes. At present the EU largely lacks mechanisms to prevent a race-to-the-bottom in tax rates and social provision. An open question is whether, and in what form, such mechanisms might emerge.

As to harmonization at the EU level, the likelihood of the Social Chapter becoming the binding floor is partly a political question. The Amsterdam Treaty still leaves the most protectionist instruments out of the EU social policy umbrella: pay, the right of association and the rights to strike and to impose lock-outs. Additionally, unanimity is required in respect of social security and social protection of workers, protection of workers against dismissal and collective bargaining and worker representation. These are the areas which probably most clearly define society's preferences in respect of labour market outcomes, and they will therefore probably continue to be regarded as properly subject to national sovereignty. Allowing an individual country to veto action in these areas, therefore, makes possible a race-to-the-bottom. In contrast to the Maastricht convergence criteria, however, which forced beneficial policy change by setting ceilings on inflation, interest rates and debt and deficits for aspiring EMU members, in the social policy area unanimity merely sets a floor and therefore does not actively encourage labour market reform (although of course it does not inhibit it).

The areas presently covered by qualified majority voting are nevertheless significant: health and safety; working conditions; information for, and consultation with, workers; equal treatment and opportunities for men and women; and integration of people excluded from the labour market. Qualified majority voting on working conditions, in particular, has some potential both for protectionism and/or preventing a race-to-the-bottom. Currently a qualified majority requires at least 62 favourable votes out of 87, i.e. 71%, so that the blocking minority is equal to 26 votes.[106] A future slump in economic activity would then provide a fertile environment for countries that wish to jointly press for social harmonization so as to prevent competition based on low labour standards.

What type of measures are likely to be approved? It is instructive to look at the four directives derived from the Agreement on Social Policy of the Maastricht Treaty – which eventually became the Social Chapter in the Amsterdam Treaty – in the light of the discussion of Chapters 2 and 3. The European works councils directive is an attempt to raise bargaining power of European labour unions by fostering their cooperation across EU countries. It is largely a reaction to the problems caused by higher capital mobility and the concomitant negative effects on the nearest poor (as in the case of the Hoover plant relocation discussed earlier). Policy-makers may then agree to directives which further curtail the ability of multinationals to relocate within the EU, by strengthening information and consultation requirements with governments and workers. Recent talk of establishing a 'code of conduct' for companies, in connection with the closure of the Renault plant at Vilvoorde in Belgium (see the press clipping at the head of this chapter), which meant dismissing 3,100 workers in favour of a greater production effort in Spain, would be a step in this direction. Under the information/consultation heading, such measures could be approved by qualified majority voting and it would therefore be difficult for a handful of governments, in particular those most likely to benefit from relocation, to veto them.

The three remaining directives strengthen the non-discriminatory stance of EU social policy, for part-time employees *vis-à-vis* full-time ones, and for women *vis-à-vis* men (both in sex discrimination cases and, since men rarely take advantage of it, also regarding parental leave). Here the interaction with economic integration is not obvious. What all three measures have in common is an attempt to foster female labour participation, though for this to have a favourable impact on unemployment the potentially adverse effects on labour demand would need to overcome. Moreover, there is a genuine lack of consensus on the best social policies across the EU, deriving from differences in national preferences, traditions and stages of development. Most EU governments, and certainly the European Commission, feel pressure from public opinion to show progress in creating a social dimension to EU integration.[107] This type of directive gives them such a chance, even if gender policies should not really be uniform across countries given taste differences and in spite of discrimination not being the most pressing of social policy issues. As a result, measures seeking further reductions in the scope for discrimination are also likely to be passed in the future. A case in point might be that of employees on fixed-term contracts *vis-à-vis* permanent employees which would, however, have significant implications for labour market flexibility.

As an alternative to EU harmonization, an undesirable consequence of individual countries embarking on labour reform may be a protectionist backlash. This could take the form of a 'Fortress Europe', but this is unlikely given commitments to the World Trade Organization, and is made even less probable by the March 1998 European Commission proposal to start talks on the creation of a free trade area with the US. The alternative danger is slower intra-EU integration. An indication of how this might happen was given by the case of the posted workers' directive, discussed in Box 3.3. In Germany, benefits for the long-term unemployed were reduced at the same time that a law was passed setting a minimum wage rate for all construction workers, including those employed by foreign sub-contractors. Ten months later the EU then approved the posted workers directive, thereby extending the same principle in the German law to the whole of the EU. This exemplifies the willingness of both individual governments and the EU to seek a politically viable combination of somewhat less integration and somewhat less social protection.

5.2.2 Good and bad ideas for a Social Chapter

From the point of view of reducing the persistently high levels of unemployment in most EU countries, increased labour market flexibility would be a welcome development. The so-called European model has involved the maintenance of both a high level of labour market rigidity and a high level of social protection; the absence of strong electoral pressure for change suggests that this choice has been a political equilibrium.[108] In an environment of increasing competition, however, this choice becomes increasingly more costly in terms of unemployment and it risks serious problems of sustainability of the Welfare State. A drive for harmonization at the EU level should not stand in the way of these reforms. On the other hand, we have seen that there are plausible arguments that make some types of social harmonization welfare improving. A set of recommendations that ensue from our discussion follows.

First, it is worth reiterating one conclusion from Chapter 3. Harmonization makes sense only at similar standards of development, and with similar social preferences between efficiency on the one hand and redistribution towards the poor on the other. Income disparities are already large among current EU members and will dramatically increase with the next enlargement to the East. There are also large disparities in labour market regulations and in the organization of social policies. Since these are present even amongst countries with similar income levels, they constitute compelling prima facie evidence for different national preferences regarding the tradeoff between efficiency and redistribution, which should be respected. Thus, the most policy-makers should strive for is minimum standards which are acceptable to all countries.

Second, fostering a dialogue between the representatives of employers and employees at the European level so that EU social policy is based on consensus is a good idea, since most measures which are harmful to a firm's ability to compete in an increasingly integrated markets will be rejected. It should be kept in mind, however, that a European federation of unions, like their national counterparts, will tend to represent employees rather than the unemployed. For example, the agreement on applying the pro-rata principle to part-time jobs implies that employees in such jobs cannot receive proportionally lower social benefits, while they might be willing to do so if the alternative were unemployment. Also, European federations of employers are more likely to represent the interests of large corporations than of small and medium-sized firms. It seems that only politicians can represent the unemployed and owners of small firms at the European level.

Lastly, our previous arguments indicate what types of social harmonization have the highest potential for welfare improvement. Let us provide some examples of desirable and undesirable measures. Most obviously, establishing a single minimum wage or a single unemployment benefit level throughout the EU would not make sense, since an average level would be too low for the richest countries and too high for the poorest ones, with the potential of causing even higher unemployment.

Measures fostering mobility are desirable, such as those suppressing any discrimination of migrant workers or any unwarranted formal or informal barriers to the mutual recognition of diplomas. By the same token, measures like the posted workers directive, which clearly deter mobility for protectionist reasons, are a bad idea. Mobility enhancing measures should, nevertheless, reduce incentives for 'benefit shopping', so as to diminish fiscal spillovers.

Measures designed to overcome problems of imperfect or asymmetric information are also potentially desirable, such as the obligation to provide representatives of workers with notice and information on collective redundancies or to foster exchanges of information among employees of multinationals in different countries. If social harmonization were to evolve into measures obstructing the shift of production sites across countries (*vide* the newspaper cutting about the Renault factory at Vilvoorde at the start of this chapter), however, then this would harm the competitiveness of firms and would be counterproductive. Problems of asymmetric information may also be overcome by regulations on health and safety, but imposing the same working conditions across countries in a way that cuts against different national tastes and customs is undesirable.

5.2.3 Enlargement to the East

Harmonizing labour conditions in the CEECs with those prevailing in some of the most advanced nations in the world is no mean task. As a result, although the EU social *acquis* is far from being a real constraint on the present EU members, it *would* constitute a binding constraint for the CEECs.

This is not so obvious from a legal point of view, since countries with a communist past have a long tradition of heavy regulation of labour issues and of devoting a high share of public expenditure to social protection (for example 31% of GDP in Poland in 1994). Moreover, the CEECs have made a big effort to adapt their legislation to EU standards in the run-up to accession decisions. As an example, Table 5.1 shows that four of the five fast-track CEECs already have regulations of collective dismissals which are comparable to those in EU countries. There exist certain gaps between national regulations and the social *acquis*, but the CEECs are not required to close all of them on accession, being able to do so in two stages. Table 5.2 summarizes the areas where the *acquis* has to be met in each stage.

Effective gaps with EU requirements do not, however, lie with the absence of legal provisions, but rather with insufficient compliance with them. Compliance with regulations implies limiting firms choices and empowering workers with certain rights. This in turn entails setting up mechanisms which enable the authorities to monitor compliance (e.g. labour inspection) and which allow workers to effectively exercise their rights (e.g. administrative and judiciary bodies). The area where the gap is widest is that of regulations on health and safety at work, because the CEECs are saddled with an inheritance of very unsatisfactory working conditions. While compliance would certainly imply important welfare gains for workers due to reductions in work-related accidents and illnesses, with attached private and public pecuniary savings, it would also entail large expenses. As a result, budgetary resources will need to be devoted to all of these activities in countries with generally narrow tax bases and already bloated social expenditures.

EU-style regulations will raise labour costs, thus reducing the demand for labour and by slowing labour relocation will be detrimental to efficiency. Not only would they imply a loss of export competitiveness, but they would also reduce the attractiveness of the CEECs for FDI. Benefits and costs have to be weighed against each other, and in this assessment the net benefits increase with income levels if, as argued earlier, these regulations are a superior good. Thus, from an efficiency point of view, the best course for the CEECs themselves would appear to be to seek to indulge in a race-to-the-bottom in respect of social protection, and, with respect to labour market reg-

Table 5.1 Employment protection regulation in Central and Eastern European countries

Country	Law	Definition of mass redundancy	Required consultation with employee representatives	Advance notice	Statutory severance pay
Czech Republic	Labour Code 1993	Redundancies resulting from changing firm objectives, new technical equipment, increasing work efficiency, other organizational changes	yes	3 months	2 months' wages unless collective agreements state otherwise
Hungary	Labour Code 1992	Dismissals of 25% of employees or at least 50 people	yes	30–90 days depending on seniority	1 months' pay if job tenure was less than 3 years, up to 6 months' pay if job tenure exceeds 25 years
Poland	Act concerning termination of employment relationships for reasons connected with establishments (1989)	Dismissals of at least 10% of the staff in establishments up to 100 workers or at least 100 workers in establishments employing more than 1000 workers	yes	45 days	1 month's pay for seniority up to 10 years, 2 months' pay for seniority of 10–20 years, 3 months' pay for seniority > 20 years + compulsory allowance for lower income workers in new job, up to 6 months
Slovenia	Law on labour relations of the Republic of Slovenia (1991)	5 workers or more	yes	6 months	Half of monthly earnings for each year of service

Sources: International Labour Organisation, *Labour Law Documents*, reproduced from Boeri, Burda and Köllö (1998) (Table 3.6), and World Bank (1997) for Slovenia.

Table 5.2 Stages of adoption of the social *acquis* in Eastern European countries

Area	First stage	Second stage
Equal opportunity for men and women	Equal pay and equal treatment in access to jobs, promotion, training and working conditions.	Equal treatment in statutory and occupational social security schemes; and for the self-employed. Protection of pregnancy and maternity at work.
Coordination of Social Security schemes	No measures needed.	Law must prevent that workers who are moving from one member state to another lose their Social Security rights.
Safety and health at work (S&H)	Employers must assess risks to S&H, make sure workers receive appropriate information and provide them with adequate training. Legislation must cover protective and preventive services, health surveillance and participation of workers in S&H issues at work.	Legislation has to comply with 13 directives containing regulations on the achievement of satisfactory levels of S&H in the most critical areas: workplace equipment, safety signs and chemical exposure.
Labour law and working conditions	Collective redundancies; employee rights in transfers of undertakings, businesses or parts of businesses, and in cases of insolvency of employers; and protection of young people at work.	Information on contract conditions; working time; information and consultation of employees through European works councils.

Source: European Commission (1994b).

ulations, to incorporate quickly only those which strengthen market mechanisms (e.g. basic workers' rights) while aiming only at a gradual adoption of measures with prohibitively expensive price tags (like health and safety) and also those making the labour market less flexible (like firing costs).

As remarked earlier, the distributional effects of the CEECs accession on the economies of present EU member states may persuade their governments to seek to impose social clauses on the CEECs in exchange for EU concessions in other fields, including direct financial support. Moreover, they have enough bargaining power in the negotiations to impose stringent conditions so that labour market regulations are effectively complied with, rather than just being nominally applicable. If these clauses are stringent, then the effect may simply be to further encourage the growth of the informal underground economy, something which should be distinctly undesirable from the view of the CEECs themselves.

6 Conclusions

Historical experience, case studies and theoretical arguments all indicate that economic integration of economies at different levels of development – while certainly an excellent idea from the point of view of economic efficiency – can have important distributional implications. In Europe these forces will impose further strain on the Western European model of social protection and labour market regulation.

We expect the dilemma to be resolved by substantial flexibility-oriented reforms. As economists, we welcome this outcome. To the extent that current labour market regulations protect the privileged position of insiders rather than the disadvantaged members of society, any reasonable economic calculus of gains and losses suggests that reform is needed regardless of developments related to integration.

A fully fledged race-to-the-bottom in labour market standards and social protection, however, should neither be expected or advocated. National systems of labour relations and social expenditure display remarkable resilience, and national differentiation of social protection schemes is fully legitimate in view of different preferences. In the light of US evidence, however, we expect important interactions among the policies of EU member states. Harmonization of minimum standards, such as those imposed by EU directives, is essential if some of the current European systems is to be preserved.

We now summarize both the general points of this report, and their particular relevance for current and prospective European integration:

- *In general.* Integration is good for the 'average' individual, but generally will have adverse effects on some individuals: Within rich countries, individuals who lose from economic integration are likely to have relatively low wealth and poor skills – whence comes an intimate relationship between economic integration and 'social policy.'

- *In Europe*. It is not surprising that 'social' aspects have been emphasized throughout the process leading to full integration, and especially when the Single Market programme and accession of relatively poor and non-homogenous countries brought integration and distribution issues to the fore.

- *In general*. Like all distribution-motivated policies, those meant to help economic disadvantaged individuals have deleterious effects on productive efficiency. Within rich countries, it makes good politico-economic sense to pursue social policy and/or limits to economic integration in order to help the 'nearest poor'.

- *In Europe*. Increased competition arising from global as well as European integration and the adoption of the single currency will have some adverse distributional consequences and encourage countries to adopt policies that inhibit integration and protect the losers (as in the Posted Workers directive). This is unfortunate, but to a degree inevitable. It would be desirable to grant full and unfettered access to EU goods markets to the CEECs as soon as possible; but full labour mobility immediately between the CEECs and the West would be undesirable, although even if this were granted, the likely policy response by Western European governments would probably limit inflows of workers from the East.

- *In general*. The coverage of social policies needs to be as extensive as possible for them to be effective. If independent policies are set for different jurisdictions within an integrated economy, only coordination can ensure they serve their intended purposes; in the absence of coordination, competition and fiscal spillovers result in a 'race-to-the-bottom.' This is to be deplored when deregulation damages individuals who are indeed worthy of protection and when it makes it impossible to redress market failures. In other words, coordination of social policies is good when policies serve a socially useful purpose.

- *In Europe*. The Social Charter and EU social policy presently feature little effective coordination, since centrally agreed constraints on national social policies are typically more restrictive than EU requirements. This need not be true in the future or in an enlarged EU: at some future point EU social policies and minimum standards will then start to constrain national policies. This is good for, as long as the EU lacks any supranational welfare system, only explicit coordination in the form of minimum standards can prevent a race-to-the-bottom.

- *In general.* Where countries are very similar then coordination may take the form of harmonization of standards, essentially extending to the integrated economy the policies that appeared optimal within each country. Where countries are very different, either in tastes or levels of development, common standards are likely to involve foregoing gains from trade as well as causing harm to the 'furthest poor', even if they do protect the poor closer to home.

- *In Europe.* Diversity is indeed desirable with respect to Central and Eastern European Countries. The CEECs should be required to introduce the full social *acquis* of the EU only gradually, and after living standards have begun to approximate those in the West; the CEECs can help themselves by ensuring that their own domestic legislation fosters the flexibility in restructuring.

- *In general.* Just because policies have distributional implications, competition among policies and the ensuing deregulation can be desirable from the point of view of many individuals and – through distorted political interactions – perhaps even for a majority of them.

- *In Europe.* Increased competition will encourage the adoption of looser national regulations and the reform of labour markets. Such increased flexibility is in any case desirable in order to help reduce European unemployment, and inherently preferable to policies that seek to inhibit integration.

Endnotes

1. See Pelkmans (1997) for a global analysis of European intergration.
2. We follow the excellent treatment in Sapir (1996). See also Blanpain and Engels (1995) for further details.
3. Implementation of the treaties may take three routes: *regulations* which apply directly to all countries; *directives* that are translated into national law, thus allowing national governments discretion on methods of implementation; and *decisions* which apply only to countries to whom they are addressed. Other dispositions, like *recommendations* and *opinions*, are not binding. Throughout this report we use the word regulation in a generic sense, not in the specific legal sense above.
4. Delpérée (1956), International Labour Office (1956) and Comité Intergouvernemental Crée par la Conférence de Messine (1956).
5. There is a precedent in the European Social Charter adopted by the Council of Europe in 1961.
6. See Grubb and Wells (1993) for rankings, and Hepple (1987) for legal details.
7. See Layard, Nickell and Jackman (1991) – Chapter 9, and Blanpain and Engels (1995).
8. See Grubb and Wells (1993).
9. Specifically, at least 10 employees for firms with 21 to 99 employees, 10% of employees for firms with 100 to 299 employees, and at least 30 employees for firms with 300 employees or more. Five individual dismissals also qualify as a collective redundancy.
10. See Hepple (1987).
11. See European Commission (1994a).
12. Case 43/75 (*Defrenne* v. *Sabena*) of April 1976.
13. See Blau and Kahn (1996).
14. See Pelkmans (1997).
15. See European Commission (1996b).
16. See European Commission (1995).
17. Roughly speaking, the price of each good under free trade (in terms of units of labour) is equal to the lowest of the two countries' prices under autarky.
18. See Baldwin and Venables (1995).
19. Ricardo himself noted that the implications of the ability to bring goods

'to the market at a reduced price' would be similar whether the development was brought about 'by the extension of foreign trade, or by improvements in machinery' (Sraffa, 1951, p. 132). His discussion of distributional implications was, however, based on a distinction between the consumption baskets of the rich and poor.

20. See Bhagwati and Kosters (1994), Wood (1994), and the papers in the Summer 1995 and Spring 1997 issues of the *Journal of Economic Perspectives*, especially Freeman (1995), Richardson (1995), Wood (1995), Topel (1997).

21. See Fortin and Lemieux (1997).

22. The distribution of wealth is much more unequal than the distribution of labour earnings.

23. Collins, O'Rourke and Williamson (1997) find that trade and migration were indeed substitutes though much of the North-Atlantic historical experience. It should be noted that the abundance and/or the quality of factors other than labour and capital, such as land, plays a role akin to that of different technologies in determing absolute advantages in production.

24. See Saint-Paul (1997) for an argument along these lines.

25. See, for example, Davis (1996) and his references for a discussion of the 'relevant' notion of factor abundance in a multicountry context.

26. For a fuller discussion of the role of labour market regulations, see Alogoskoufis *et al.* (1995).

27. Assuming physical and human capital are complements.

28. See Brown, Deardorff and Stern (1996).

29. In developed countries tariffs are generally not an efficient means of raising revenues; see Rodrik (1995) for a survey of recent contributions to the political economy of trade policy.

30. See Rodrik (1995) and Neven (1995).

31. See Sapir (1996).

32. 'The Spice Girls, Britain's five-girl pop sensation, have become tax exiles in the south of France [...] to avoid a tax bill of £32 million' ['People', *International Herald Tribune*, 26 September, 1997.] Obviously not all types of labour are equally affected by national taxes!

33. See Davis and Henrekson (1997).

34. See Saint-Paul (1997).

35. Even though the distributional consequences of EU integration and enlargement are certainly not as dramatic as those associated with trade with third-world countries, it is helpful to keep the larger picture in mind when discussing the implications of EU integration and enlargement simply because the *issues* are so similar.

36. The papers in Bhagwati and Hudec (1996) offer a clear discussion of the doubtful morality of imposing Western standards on developing countries.

37. See Sapir (1996) and our own discussion in the text and Box 3.1.

38. See Rodrik (1997).

39. See Deakin and Wilkinson (1994).

40. It should be recognized that current attempts in France and Italy to reduce working time are not prompted by distributional concerns, but are primarily an attempt to tackle high unemployment. The advocates of working-time reduction see it rather as substitute for aggregate demand management in an environment where expansionary macroeconomic policies are impossible, because of the need to maintain the exchange rate and to continue the process of fiscal retrenchment in the run up to EMU. Here, too, however, international substitution would reduce the efficacy of the legislation.

41. See Hepple (1997).

42. See Rodrik (1995).

43. See Alogoskoufis *et al.* (1995) for further discussion of this issue.

44. While regulatory failure may well be as pervasive in reality as market failures, competition among rules achieves efficient outcomes – along the lines of Tiebout (1956) – only in special circumstances, and most obviously in the absence of the very same market failures that regulation is meant to address. See Gatsios and Holmes (1997) for a well reasoned argument along these lines and further references.

45. See Slemrod (1995).

46. See Wildasin (1991) for more on tax spillovers.

47. By contrast, in the EU income tax rates are both high and vary significantly across countries, as do national VAT rates which are supposed to be harmonized at around 20%, although numerous exceptions are allowed.

48. See Gruber and Madrian (1994), Holtz-Eakin (1994) and Monheit and Cooper (1994).

49. See Peterson and Rom (1990).

50. Figures are from European Commission (1997).

51. OECD (1994) provides graphical evidence to suggest that there is less FDI to countries with stringent regulations. De Menil (1998) provides econometric evidence from a large cross-country panel of firms that suggests a statistically significant inverse relationship between the average rate of return (above German long bonds) and a measure of the strength of labour dismissal laws.

52. See, for example, Krugman (1991) and Krugman and Obstfeld (1997).

53. See European Commission (1996a).

54. See Sapir (1996) or Pelkmans (1997).

55. See OECD (1996).

56. See Graham and Krugman (1993) for a survey.

57. See Dunning (1993).

58. See Brainard (1993b).

59. See Brainard (1993a).

60. See European Commission (1996b).

61. See European Commission (1998a).

62. See Cummins and Hubbard (1995).

63. See European Commission (1998b).

64. This follows Boeri *et al.* (1998) and Baldwin *et al.* (1997). Reviews of the consequences of accession for these four countries can be found in Bliss and Braga de Macedo (1990) and Krugman (1997).

65. Using a Hodrick-Prescott filter.
66. See O'Grada and O'Rourke (1994).
67. See Bentolila and Dolado (1994).
68. See Bover *et al.* (1998c).
69. See Bover *et al.* (1998a) for further information on the similarities and differences in Portuguese and Spanish labour markets.
70. See Esteban (1997).
71. The European Commission argues that its criteria for choosing the first group are based on objective assessments of the applicants. To join the EU, a country must have stable institutions guaranteeing democracy, the rule of law, human rights and protection of minorities, a functioning market economy; and the ability to accept the obligations of membership, including the aims of political, economic and monetary union.
72. See Boeri *et al* (1998).
73. For surveys on the consequences of Eastern enlargement see Baldwin *et al.* (1995) and Faini and Portes (1995).
74. See Baldwin *et al.*
75. See Bentolila (1997) for Poland; and World Bank (1997) for Slovenia.
76. See Akerlof *et al.* (1991). The 1:1 conversion rate between the Ost Mark and Deutsche Mark has sometimes been blamed for Germany's unification problems, but this is not very compelling: while much of East German industry might have been viable at a 10:1 rate it is unlikely that East Germans would have accepted the implied differentials with West German living standards; the result would then have been wage inflation in the East together with massive East-to-West migration (see Bean, 1992).
77. See Krugman and Venables (1995).
78. Bentolila (1997) compares Poland and Spain from the point of view of EU accession.
79. See 'Poland prepares for Europe', *The Economist*, 20/26 September 1997.
80. See Gros and Gociarz (1996).
81. See Alogoskoufis *et al.* (1995) and the references therein.
82. See Topel (1997).
83. See Bover *et al.* (1998b) and Sastre (1997).
84. See Bentolila and Dolado (1994) and Saint-Psul (1996).
85. See Bertola and Ichino (1995).
86. See Dolado *et al.* (1996).
87. See OECD (1997b).
88. See European Commission (1995).
89. See European Commission (1995).
90. See Begg *et al.* (1993).
91. See OECD (1997a).
92. See European Commission (1997).
93. These data refer to Eurostat's NUTS1 classification, which breaks the EU down into 77 regions, and includes only the nine EU countries for which data are available (i.e. it omits Austria, Denmark, Greece, Ireland, Luxembourg and Portugal).
94. See Faini (1996).

95. 'Millions want to come', *The Economist*, 4 April 1998.
96. See Bean (1992).
97. See Krugman (1991).
98. This is what Frankel and Rose (1996) find with disaggregated data over the period 1959–93.
99. Buiter and Sibert (1997).
100. Some unemployment is desirable to ensure that workers can be matched to the appropriate jobs.
101. See Sibert and Sutherland (1997).
102. See Calmfors and Drifill (1988).
103. See Danthine and Hunt (1994).
104. See European Commission (1996b).
105. See Buti *et al.* (1998).
106. Votes of members are weighted as follows: Austria (4), Belgium (5), Denmark (3), Finland (3), France (10), Germany (10), Greece (5), Ireland (3), Italy (10), Luxembourg (2), Netherlands (5), Portugal (5), Spain (8), Sweden (4), UK (10).
107. It is quite significant that in its web page (http//www.eu.int) explanation of the Amsterdam Treaty, the Commission provides a long answer to the question 'We have heard a lot about "Social Europe" – what progress is being made in this area on the basis of the Treaty?'. We may also note in passing that the next one is: 'What does the Treaty do to offset the negative effects of economic globalization?'
108. See Alogoskoufis *et al.* (1995).

References

Akerlof, G., A. Rose, J. Yellen and H. Hessenius (1991) 'East Germany in from the cold: the economic aftermath of currency union', *Brookings Papers on Economic Activity* 1, 1–87.

Alogoskoufis, G., C. Bean, G. Bertola, D. Cohen, J. J. Dolado and G. Saint-Paul (1995) *Monitoring European Integration 5: Unemployment Choices for Europe*, London: Centre for Economic Policy Research.

Baldwin, R., J. Francois and R. Portes (1997) 'The costs and benefits of Eastern enlargement: The impact on the EU and Central Europe', *Economic Policy* 24, 125–70.

Baldwin, R., P. Haaparanta and J. Kiander (eds.) (1995) *Expanding Membership of the European Union*, Cambridge: Cambridge University Press.

Baldwin, R. and A. Venables (1995) 'Regional economic integration', in G. Grossman and K. Rogoff (eds.) *Handbook of International Economics* Vol. 3, Amsterdam: North-Holland.

Bean, C. (1992) 'Economic and monetary union in Europe', *Journal of Economic Perspectives* 6, Fall, 31–52.

Begg, D., J. Cremer, J-P. Danthine, J. Edwards, V. Grilli, D. Neven, P. Seabright, H-W. Sinn, A. Venables and C. Wyplosz (1993) *Monitoring European Integration 4: Making sense of subsidiarity: How much centralization for Europe?*', London: Centre of Economic Policy Research.

Bentolila, S. (1997) 'Polish labour market institutions on the road to the EU', CEMFI Working Paper 9712.

Bentolila, S. and J. J. Dolado (1994) 'Labour flexibility and wages: lessons from Spain', *Economic Policy* 18, 53–99.

Bertola, G. and A. Ichino (1995) 'Crossing the river: A comparative perspective on Italian employment dynamics', *Economic Policy* 21, 359–420.

Bhagwati, J. and R. E. Hudec (eds.) (1996) *Fair Trade and Harmonization*, Cambridge, Mass: MIT Press.

Bhagwati, J. and M. H. Kosters (eds.) (1994) *Trade and Wages: Levelling wages down?*, Washington DC: AEI Press.

Blanpain, R. and C. Engels (1995) *European Labour Law*, 3rd edn, Deventer: Kluwer Law and Taxation Publishers.

Blau, F. D. and L. M. Kahn (1996) 'Wage structure and gender earnings differentials: an international comparison', *Economica* 63, S29–S62.

Bliss, C. and J. Braga de Macedo (eds.) (1990) *Unity and Diversity in the European Economy*, Cambridge: Cambridge University Press.

Boeri, T., M. Burda and J. Köllö (1998) *Labour markets in the transition economies of Central and Eastern Europe*, London: Centre for Economic Policy Research.

Bover, O., P. Garcia-Perea and P. Portugal (1998a) 'A comparative study of the Portuguese and Spanish labour markets', Working Paper 9807, Bank of Spain, Research Department.

Bover, O., M. Arellano and S. Bentolila (1998b) 'The distribution of earnings in Spain during the 1980s: The effects of skill, unemployment, and union power', Centro de Estudios Monetarios y Financieros, mimeo.

Bover, O., M. Arellano and S. Bentolila (1998c) 'Unemployment duration, benefit duration and the business cycle', Working Paper 1840, London: Centre for Economic Policy Research.

Brainard, S. L. (1993a) 'An empirical assessment of the proximity-concentration trade-off between multinational sales and trade', NBER Working Paper 4580.

Brainard, S. L. (1993b) 'A simple theory of multinational corporations and trade with a trade-off between multinational sales and trade', NBER Working Paper 4269.

Brown, D. K., A. V. Deardorff and R. M. Stern (1996) 'International labour standards and trade: A theoretical analysis', in J. Bhagwati and R. E. Hudec (eds.) *Fair Trade and Harmonization: Prerequisites for Free Trade?*, Cambridge, Mass: MIT Press, 227–80.

Buiter, W. H. and A. C. Sibert (1997) 'Transition issues for the European monetary union', Discussion Paper 1728, London: Centre for Economic Policy Research.

Buti, M., L. R. Pench and P. Sestito (1998) 'Contending theories and institutional complexities', European Investment Bank, Report 98/01.

Calmfors, L. and J. Driffill (1988) 'Bargaining Structure, Corporatism and Macroeconomic Performance', *Economic Policy* 6, 14–61.

Collins, W. J., K. H. O'Rourke and J. G. Williamson (1997) 'Were Trade and Factor Mobility Substitutes in History?' Discussion Paper 1661; forthcoming in: G. de Melo, R. Faini and K. Zimmerman (eds.) *Trade and Factor Mobility*, Cambridge: Cambridge University Press.

Comité Intergouvernemental Crée par la Conférence de Messine (1956) *Rapport de Chefs de Délégation aux Ministres des Affaires Etrangéres*, Brussels.

Cummins, J. G. and R. G. Hubbard (1995) 'Is Foreign Direct Investment Sensitive to Taxes?' in M. Feldstein, J. Hines and R.G. Hubbard (eds.) *Taxing Multinational Corporations*, Chicago: University of Chicago Press.

Danthine, J. P. and J. Hunt (1994) 'Wage Bargaining Structure, Employment and Economic Integration', *Economic Journal* 104, 528–41.

Davies, P. (1997) 'Posted workers: Single Market or protection of national labour law systems?' *Common Market Law Review* 34(3), 571–602.

Davis, D. R. (1996) 'Trade Liberalization and Income Distribution' NBER working paper 5693.

Davis, S. J. and M. Henrekson (1997) 'Industrial Policy, Employer Size, and Economic Performance in Sweden' in R.B. Freeman, R. Topel and B. Swedenborg (eds.) *The Welfare State in Transition: Reforming the Swedish model*, Chicago: University of Chicago Press for the NBER.

Deakin, S. and F. Wilkinson (1994) 'Rights vs Efficiency? The economic case for transnational labour standards' *Industrial Law Journal* 23, 289–310.

Delpérée, A. (1956) *Politique sociale et intégration economique*, Liége: Georges Thone.

De Menil, G. (1998), 'Capital market integration in the EU: How far has it gone?', presented at the 27th *Economic Policy* Panel meeting, London.

Dolado, J. J., F. Kramarz, S. Machin, A. Manning, D. Margolis and C. Teulings (1996), 'The economic impact of minimum wages', *Economic Policy*, 23, 317–72.

Dunning, J. (1993), *The globalization of business: The challenge of the 1990s*, London: Routledge.

Esteban, J. M. (1997) 'An analysis of inter-regional inequalities in Europe during the 1980s', Barcelona: Instituto de Análisis Económico mimeo.

European Commission (1994a) 'European Social Policy. A way forward for the Union', COM(94) 333, Brussels.

European Commission (1994b), 'White Paper. Preparation of the Associated Countries of Central and Eastern Europe for Integration into the Internal Market of the Union', Annex: COM(94) 361/3, Brussels.

European Commission (1995) 'Social Protection in Europe 1995' COM(95) 457 final, Brussels.

European Commission (1996a) 'Economic Evaluation of the Internal Market', *European Economy*, 4.

European Commission (1996b) 'The 1996 Single Market Review', SEC(96) 2378, Brussels.

European Commission (1997) *Employment in Europe 1997*, Luxembourg.

European Commission (1998a) *Foreign Direct Investment*, The Single Market Review sub-series IV, Vol. 1, London: Kogan Page.

European Commission (1998b) *Trade patterns inside the Single Market*, The Single Market Review sub-series IV, Vol. 2, London: Kogan Page.

Eurostat (1997) *Labour Costs Survey*, Luxembourg.

Faini, R. (1996) 'European Migrants. An Endangered Species?', Università di Brescia, mimeo.

Faini, R. and R. Portes (eds.) (1995) *EU Trade with Eastern Europe: Adjustment and Opportunities*, London: Centre for Economic Policy Research.

Fortin, N. and T. Lemieux (1997) 'Institutional Changes and Rising Wage Inequality: Is There a Linkage?' *Journal of Economic Perspectives* 11(2), 75–96.

Frankel, J. A. and A. K. Rose (1996) 'The Endogeneity of the Optimum Currency Area Criteria', Discussion Paper 1473, London: Centre for Economic Policy Research.

Freeman, R. (1995) 'Are your wages set in Bejing?', *Journal of Economic Perspectives* 9(3) 15–32.

Gatsios, K. and P. Holmes (1997) 'International Competition and International Harmonization', Global Economic Institutions Working Paper Series No. 37, forthcoming in *New Palgrave Dictionary of Law and Economics*.

Graham, E. and P. Krugman (1993) 'The surge in foreign direct investment in the 1980s', in K. Froot (ed.) *Foreign Direct Investment*, Chicago and London, University of Chicago Press.

Gros, D. and A. Gociarz (1996) 'A note on the trade potential of Central and Eastern Europe', *European Journal of Political Economy* 12.

Grubb, D. and W. Wells (1993) 'Employment Regulation and Patterns of Work in EC Countries', *OECD Economic Studies* 21, Winter, 7–58.

Gruber, J. and B. C. Madrian (1994) 'Health Insurance and Mobility: the effects of public policy on job-lock', *Industrial and Labour Relations Review*, 48(1), October, 86–102.

Hepple, B. (1987) 'Security of Employment' in R. Blanpain (ed.), *Comparative Labour Law and Industrial Relations*, 3rd edn, Deventer: Kluwer Law and Taxation Publishers.

Hepple, B. (1997) 'New Approaches to International Labour Regulation', *Industrial Law Journal*, 26(4), December, 353–66.

Holtz-Eakin, D. (1994) 'Health Insurance Provision and Labour Market Efficiency in the United States and Germany', Chapter 6 in R. M. Blank (ed.) *Social Protection vs. Economic Flexibility: Is there a tradeoff?*, Chicago and London: Chicago University Press.

International Labour Office (1956) *Social aspects of European economic co-operation. Report by a group of experts*, Geneva.

Krugman, P. (1991) *Geography and Trade*, Cambridge, Mass: MIT Press.

Krugman, P. (1997), 'Good News from Ireland: A geographical perspective' in Gray, A. (de) *International Perspectives on the Irish Economy*, Dublin: Inderon.

Krugman, P. and M. Obstfeld (1997) *International Economics: Theory and Policy*, 4th edn., Reading, Mass: Addison-Wesley.

Krugman, P. and A. Venables (1995) 'Globalisation and the inequality of nations' *Quarterly Journal of Economics*, 110, 857–80.

Layard, R., S. Nickell and R. Jackman (1991) *Unemployment. Macroeconomic Performance and the Labour Market*, Oxford: Oxford University Press.

Monheit, A. C. and P. F. Cooper (1994) 'Health Insurance and Job Mobility: theory and evidence', *Industrial and Labour Relations Review* 48(1), October, 68–85.

Neven, D. (1995) 'Trade Liberalization with Eastern Nations: How Sensitive?' in R. Faini and R. Portes (eds.) (1995) *EU Trade with Eastern Europe: Adjustment and Opportunities*, London: Centre for Economic Policy Research.

OECD (1994) *Employment Outlook 1994*, Paris.

OECD (1996) *International Direct Investment Statistics Yearbook*, Paris.

OECD (1997a) *Implementing the OECD Jobs Strategy: Member Countries' Experience*, Paris.

OECD (1997b) 'Economic Performance and the Structure of Collective Bargaining', *Employment Outlook*, Paris

O'Grada, C. and K. O'Rourke (1994), 'Irish economic growth, 1945–88', Discussion Paper 975, London: Centre for Economic Policy Research.

Pelkmans, J. (1997) *European Integration. Methods and Economic Analysis*, Harlow: Addison Wesley Longman.

Peterson, P. E. and M. Rom (1990) *'Welfare Magnets: A New Case for National Standards'*, Washington DC, The Brookings Institution.

Richardson, J. D. (1995) 'Income Inequality and Trade: How to Think, What to Conclude', *Journal of Economic Perspectives* 9(3), 33–56.

Rodrik, D. (1995) 'Political Economy of Trade Policy' in G. Grossman and K. Rogoff (eds.), *Handbook of International Economics*, Vol. 3, Amsterdam, North-Holland.

Rodrik, D. (1997) 'Trade, Social Insurance, and the Limits to Globalization' NBER Working Paper 5905.

Saint-Paul, G. (1996) 'Exploring the Political Economy of Labour Market Institutions', *Economic Policy* 23, 263–315.

Saint-Paul, G. (1997) 'Economic Integration, Factor Mobility, and Wage Convergence', *International Tax and Public Finance* 4(3), July, 291–306.

Sapir, A. (1996) 'Trade Liberalization and the Harmonization of Social Policies: Lessons from European Integration', in J. Bhagwati and R. E. Hudec (eds.) *Fair Trade and Harmonization. Prerequisites for Free Trade?*, Cambridge, Mass: MIT Press, 543–70.

Sastre, M. (1997) 'Essays on the measurement of inequality in Spain', Madrid: Universidad Complutense, mimeo.

Sibert, A. C. and A. Sutherland (1997) 'Monetary Regimes and Labour Market Reform', Discussion Paper 1731, Centre for Economic Policy Research.

Slemrod, J. (1995) 'Tax Cacophony and the Benefits of Free Trade' in J. Bhagwati and R. E. Hudec (eds.) *Fair Trade and Harmonization. Prerequisites for Free Trade?*, Cambridge Mass: MIT Press.

Sraffa, P. (ed.) (1951) *The works and correspondence of David Ricardo: On the principles of political economy and taxation*, Vol.1, Cambridge: Cambridge University Press.

Tiebout, C. M. (1956) 'A pure theory of local expenditure', *Journal of Political Economy* 64(5), 416–24.

Topel, R. (1997) 'Factor proportions and Relative Wages: The Supply-Side Determinants of Wage Inequality' *Journal of Economic Perspectives* 11, 55–74.

Wildasin, D. E. (1991) 'Income Redistribution in a Common market', *American Economic Review* 81(4), 757–75.

Wood, A. (1994) *North-South Trade, Employment, and Inequality: Changing fortunes in a skill-driven world*, Oxford: Clarendon Press / New York: Oxford University Press.

Wood, A. (1995) 'How Trade Hurt Unskilled Workers', *Journal of Economic Perspectives* 9(3), 57–80.

World Bank (1997) 'Slovenia. Labour Market Issues', Europe and Central Asia Regional Office, mimeo.